Worshipping God

Devoting our lives to His glory

R. T. Kendall

Hodder & Stoughton
LONDON SYDNEY AUCKLAND

Copyright © 1989 R. T. Kendall
Preface © 1999 R. T. Kendall
Foreword © 1999 Darlene Zschech

First published in Great Britain in 1989
This edition 2004

British Library Cataloguing in Publication Data
A record for this book is available from the British Library

ISBN 0 340 86332 3

Typeset by Avon Dataset Ltd, Bidford-on-Avon, Warks

Printed and bound in Great Britain by
Clays Ltd, St Ives plc

The paper and board used in this paperback are natural recyclable products made from wood grown in sustainable forests. The manufacturing processes conform to the environmental regulations of the country of origin.

Hodder & Stoughton
A Division of Hodder Headline Ltd
338 Euston Road
London NW1 3BH
www.madaboutbooks.com

To Meint and Linda
Brad, Brent and Bryce

FOREWORD

About twelve months ago, I found myself reading this book, *Worshipping God*, loving the content, loving the challenge and loving the truths for the Word that was revealed within its pages. I wondered about its author and hoped one day we'd meet. The next day, I went to my office and found a fax from R. T. Kendall inviting me to minister at Westminster Chapel in London!

Coincidence, you may say, but I believe God orchestrates these moments for *his* purposes, which one day we may see revealed.

I have seen R. T.'s heart for the local church and his revelation on the power of worship affecting many lives. I really believe that God is restoring worship to *his* Church, all over the world, *in spirit and in truth*.

The spiritual temperature is certainly hotting up and I've heard of and been to hundreds of churches worldwide that say: 'We were never a worshipping church, but the hunger for more of Christ has caused us to become one.'

Gone are the days of just singing a couple of songs while the late people walk in, or going through the motions of singing some of our old favourites. God is causing his Church to *worship* him with our lives: living a lifestyle of love, and lifting our hearts and voices together in song, experiencing depth and heights in the presence of our precious Lord like never before. There is a wave of praise and worship coming – a new sound, a new song, a unified sound as the Church comes together to bless our magnificent Lord.

So, all of you who live to draw closer to our Lord, who love to worship him: *enjoy this book!*

Let it speak to your heart.

Darlene Zschech
Hills Christian Life Centre
NSW, Australia

PREFACE

I am not an expert on the subject of worship. I never dreamed that I would write a book on this subject.

What happened was this. I began preaching from Philippians in January 1985. During the autumn of 1986, when we were still using the Authorised Version, we reached Philippians 3:3: 'We are the circumcision who worship God in the Spirit.' I planned to preach a sermon on worship. In translating the Greek I found that Paul actually said, 'We worship by the Spirit of God', that is, by the impulse of the Spirit.

I felt that a second sermon was needed. But when I finished it various members of the congregation urged me to go on with this subject. I agreed to a third sermon. I was not prepared for the excitement I myself felt, and I think others as well. I kept going and the series exceeded the number of chapters of this book.

In 1995 Paul Cain preached a sermon on the subject of worship that was epoch-making. It did more to change our church generally and my own life particularly than any other sermon I have listened to in years and years. The funny thing is, this book was written *before* Paul Cain came to us. His influence on us in this area only accentuated all I said. Nothing I wrote needed changing; I can only say I believe all I wrote then twice as much now!

A host of friends have kindly commended this book, and I thank them most warmly. I am especially thankful to Darlene Zschech for her Foreword. I had to pinch myself on a memorable Sunday evening in May 1998 when she led us in worship at Westminster, singing 'Shout to the Lord'; it seemed too good to be true. It showed how far the Chapel has come since I wrote this book and yet how the exposition of God's unchanging word remains the same.

When I first began bonefishing on Largo Sound in 1964 I could not have known that one day my family and I would be offered the use of a home right on that tropical paradise. Captain and Mrs Meint Huesman began turning their home, boat and car over to us in 1984. Never have we had such friends. I gratefully and affectionately dedicate this volume to them and their three sons.

In the meantime I have improved my bonefishing skills. But one of my greatest thrills was to lead Don Gurgiolo to Christ in the summer of 1982 (see Introduction). I can also now regard a number of professional bonefish guides as friends! Jack Brothers (now in Heaven), Harry Spear, Oz Keagy and John Sutter have repeatedly taken me fishing in exchange for my teaching them more about the Bible as we fish – and worship – together.

R. T. Kendall
London
February 1999

INTRODUCTION

There is an old story about two churches in Alabama – one Baptist, the other Methodist – that were located across the street from each other. Both were holding a 'revival' at the same time. Sadly, a rivalry had developed between the two churches over the years, partly due to theological differences. The 'revival' at any rate came and went. Later some Baptists were heard to comment, 'Well, we didn't have much of a revival, but thank God the Methodists didn't either.'

In America the word revival is used hastily and uncritically to describe what in Britain we prefer to call a mission. Revival, strictly speaking, is indeed too often the wrong word, particularly when authentic revival doesn't come. But it is not surprising that real revival doesn't come when there is such a rivalry and competitive spirit as I just described. The Holy Spirit is surely grieved.

But I suspect that the British too have their Achilles' heel when it comes to the use of a word: worship. How often have I heard the phrase, 'We are going to have a time of worship', when all that really happens is a time of singing hymns or choruses. I fear that worship no more takes place than revival does! And yet it is not surprising that real worship doesn't take place, and that is why I have written this book.

Worship is only really done by the Holy Spirit. As genuine revival only comes by the Holy Spirit so too does true worship. The Holy Spirit is as essential to one as the other.

To illustrate this crucial point let me share my favourite

sermon illustration with you. My hobby is bonefishing. A man once came into my vestry and asked, 'What is bonefishing?' Jokingly I replied, 'It is a requirement for membership of Westminster Chapel!'

Bonefishing is a shallow water sport that is done in the tropical, clear waters of the sea. The only place it is found in the United States is in the Florida Keys, a string of small islands between Miami and Key West. The bonefish (so named because it is full of bones and largely inedible) is a wily, skittish but very powerful fish, caught with a rod and reel, averaging between five and ten pounds. It is usually caught by simultaneous hunting and fishing. You literally stalk them in inches of water near the shore-lines. The ideal depth of water is between the ankle and knee. One of the best ways to catch them is to wade for them, providing you do so discreetly and quietly. For if they see you before you see them they explode in nervous fear and take off like a discharged torpedo. By then it is too late to catch them. One usually needs a professional guide to locate and catch them. A real sportsman more-over releases all his fish unharmed.

I had heard a lot about bonefishing, especially when my wife and I would travel to the Keys for other kinds of fishing. The more I heard and read about bonefishing the more I wanted to give it a try. It began in 1964. I decided to rent a boat at Gilbert's Fishing Camp at Jewfish Creek, just north of Key Largo. I said to the manager, 'I want to go bonefishing.' He said, 'Fine, who is your guide?' I said, 'I don't need a guide.'

'Are you a bonefisherman?'

'I will be after today.'

'Have you ever been bonefishing before?'

'No.'

'Nobody – nobody but a fool – goes bonefishing with-out a guide', the manager warned me.

'Will you please rent me a boat?' I asked.

'Sure, I'll rent you a boat.'

'Will you show me on the map where to go?'

He obliged. 'Go out across Blackwater Sound, then go through this small cut that takes you into Largo Sound. On the other side of the shoreline there are plenty of bonefish.' I had my rod and reel and plenty of live shrimp for bait. I went out about ten o'clock in the morning.

When I returned just before sundown the fishing camp manager asked, 'How many did you catch?'

'There weren't any', I replied with no little chagrin.

'Go look over there and look in that ice chest', he said. In that chest was a huge ten-pound bonefish that someone had caught earlier that day. It was waiting to be collected by a taxidermist, for a lot of people pay to have their first bonefish mounted as a trophy to remind them of their proud accomplishment.

It almost made me sick with envy. 'Where was that fish caught?' I asked. 'Largo Sound', came the reply. The man who actually caught that big bonefish overheard us talking. He said to me, 'We saw you in Largo Sound. There were bonefish all over the place. Didn't you see them?'

The camp manager laughed. 'I told you that you should have a guide.'

Never in my life was I so frustrated, not to say humbled. I did not hire a professional guide because I didn't want to pay their fee and I wanted particularly to demonstrate that I was such an exceptional fisherman that I could bring in a bonefish all by myself without the help of a guide.

I refused to give in. I read all the articles on bonefishing from fishing magazines I could get my hands on. I returned to the same place the following week, fully prepared to catch my first bonefish without the assistance of a guide.

But it was a repeat performance. So was the week after that. I am too embarrassed to tell you how many weeks – and months – I went to Largo Sound, only to return at the end of the day without catching, or even seeing, my first bonefish. I spent far more money on boat rentals than the professional guide would have cost. And my pride had been dealt with as well.

I finally gave in. 'Find me the best guide in the Keys', I ordered. 'The man you want is Don Gurgiolo'. I phoned him and booked him. 'Where do I meet you?' I asked. 'Largo Sound', came the reply. I was disappointed. I wanted to go where there were bonefish. But we headed straight across to the other side of Largo Sound. 'There are no fish here', I said unwisely. He turned off the motor and began 'poling' the boat. (I experienced the nearest equivalent to poling when I took my family punting on the Cherwell in Oxford.)

'Shh, look over there – eighty feet at ten o'clock (the bow of the boat being twelve) – a nine pound bonefish', Don whispered with excitement after only five minutes.

'Where? I don't see anything.'

'It's too late now, he's gone. Don't worry, there'll be another.'

There was, but I missed him too.

'Relax, Kendall. Do you see that white spot at two o'clock? Keep your eyes on that spot. The fish isn't there yet, he's at twelve o'clock, two hundred feet away. He's coming toward one. Now he's at two o'clock. See him?'

I did. 'So that's a bonefish!', I muttered. Before the day was over I was able to see them. We actually hooked five by the time we had to return to the dock.

What made the difference? The guide.

Jesus said of the Holy Spirit, 'He will guide you into all truth' (John 16:13). Without the Spirit's help we cannot grasp spiritual truth. The natural man receiveth not the things of the Spirit of God', said Paul (1 Cor. 2: 14), for 'they are foolishness unto him: neither can he know them, because they are spiritually discerned.' We may think we can grasp the Bible and the things of the Spirit without the Spirit but such thinking is utter folly. The truth is there, but we will not see it or grasp it until we humbly depend on the Spirit to help us.

So too with worshipping God.

CONTENTS

CHAPTER 1

SPIRIT-FILLED WORSHIP

'For we are the circumcision, which worship God in the spirit, and rejoice in Christ Jesus, and have no confidence in the flesh.' (Philippians 3:3)

I believe that every Christian has one fundamental calling and one primary duty – a duty which is also a delight. We are called, by the way we live and in all we do, to worship God. This is a full-time activity, not only here on earth, but in heaven, too.

Every church, therefore, must ask one basic question: how can our services lead the people out in a spirit of worship? A church should not be preoccupied with perpetuating a certain tradition, or be looking over its shoulder to see what others are doing. Instead, it should be asking, 'How do we conduct services that are honouring to God?' This is the important thing, no matter who may be offended as a result.

But what exactly is worship? How do we worship God? What is involved? In Philippians 3:3 Paul says that 'we . . . worship God in the spirit', or – as the NIV translates it – 'by the spirit of God' (the Greek means those 'who serve under the impulse of the Spirit of God'). I believe that the key to understanding and experiencing worship lies in this verse. True worship is in the Spirit or by the Spirit of God.

Two Greek words in the New Testament are translated by our word 'worship'. One is *proskuneo*, which is used sixty times and means 'to adore', 'to give reverence to'. This refers to the condition of the heart. It is the word used by Jesus when he said to the woman of Samaria, 'God is a Spirit: and they that worship him must worship him in spirit and in truth' (John 4:24).

The other word is *latreuontes,* which appears as a noun or a verb twenty-six times, and may be translated as 'service'. This is the word which is used to refer to public worship, and comes in Philippians 3:3: '. . . who *serve* (worship) God in the spirit.' Thus both words are used in the context of Spirit-led and Spirit-controlled worship.

In this first chapter I want to give a definition of worship and show what the design, or aim, of worship is. I then want to deal with doubtful worship and finally give a description of dynamic worship.

Here, then, is my own definition of worship: it is the response to, and/or preparation for, the preached word. I say this, not because I am trying to defend the Reformed tradition, or because I want to perpetuate any church's tradition as a preaching centre, but because I happen to be convinced that worship as described in the New Testament makes preaching central.

I think everyone would agree that the greatest service that has ever been held took place on the Day of Pentecost. Acts 2:42 gives us a description of the pattern of the earliest known Christian worship. We read: 'And they continued stedfastly in the apostles' doctrine and fellowship, and in breaking of bread, and in prayers.' This was obviously in response to the preached word.

What, then, is the role of the Spirit in worship? As we have seen, in John 4:24 Jesus said, 'God is a Spirit, and they that worship him must worship him in spirit and in truth'. The Spirit always comes first. In worship, the Spirit prepares our minds and hearts to receive God's word, and, as we see at Pentecost, it is the Spirit who brings about a change of heart and enables us to continue in the apostles' doctrine.

Incidentally, some people set great store by the building in which they worship. Perhaps the woman of Samaria was one of these, for she said, 'Our fathers worshipped in this mountain' (John 4:20). But when Jesus said, 'God is a Spirit, and they that worship him must worship him in spirit and in truth,' he was telling us that the place and building are not important.

But if the first thing is the Spirit, what is the role of the truth? Truth – Christian doctrine as revealed in the word of God – is the proof and guarantee that one is in the Spirit; it also serves as a yardstick for testing actions which are allegedly in the Spirit but which in fact are not. The truth keeps worship from going off the rails. The Bible was not given to replace the Holy Spirit. The Bible is there to correct abuse, and to help us make sure that our worship and our Christian walk are genuinely in the Spirit.

The object of our worship is, of course, the triune God. Look again at Philippians 3:3: 'We . . . worship God in the spirit, and rejoice in Christ Jesus.' Worship centres on God, with special attention given to praising God for Jesus – for who he is and what he has done.

A. W. Tozer, in his book *Whatever Happened to Worship?*, quotes Dr George Watson, who said there are two levels in the worship of God: gratitude and excellence. He went on to say that most people never get beyond the level of gratitude; few worship God for his excellence, for all that he is, for his transcendent and immanent glory.

When we think of God's transcendence, we usually think of the glory of God. Many of our hymns praise God for his majesty, glory and the awefulness of his throne. And to some people, this aspect of God is all that matters. But there is another side to the worship of God. Paul said, 'Because ye are sons, God hath sent forth the Spirit of his Son into your hearts, crying, Abba, Father' (Gal. 4:6). And in Romans 8:16 Paul said, 'The Spirit himself beareth witness with our spirit, that we are the children of God.' This is the most intimate language. 'Abba, Father' literally means (I almost blush to use it) – 'Daddy'.

Many of us are so sophisticated that the only kind of worship we can envisage is that which deals with the transcendence of God, and we are offended by some of the more intimate choruses. But we need to realise that it is just as honouring to God to praise him for his immanence as it is to praise him for his transcendence. By God's immanence, I mean the wonderful way he works within nature, within our world and daily events, and deep within our lives. I mean his closeness to us. One Sunday someone came to me and said, 'Dr Kendall, I want to share something with you. I was praying recently and I felt that God was asking me to put my arms around him. So I did – I just stood up and put my arms around the Lord. And the warmest feeling came over me.' Now that story may offend some people, but it didn't offend me.

This leads me on to look at the aim of our worship. Our aim should be to glorify God and edify the soul of every person present. It's easy to talk about glorifying God, but what does it mean? Someone may say, 'It's being sound in your doctrine and singing hymns about God's glory.' But that is too superficial an answer. To glorify God means to please him. We must continually ask ourselves this very searching question: when we meet together to worship God, is it our aim to please him or to please ourselves?

I know that the answer here can be 'both', and in the end that is true. But we will never succeed in pleasing God until we forget about ourselves. There is a parallel, here, with buying presents. There are two ways of buying presents. We can think, 'Oh, I've got to buy so-and-so a present or they'll wonder why I didn't.' And we just buy any old thing. Or we can take our time because we want to get a present which will thrill the recipient. We don't just choose something that *we* would like to be given, but we buy what we hope will give pleasure to the other person. For the joy of giving is in making someone else happy.

And it is the same with worship. We want to bring joy to God. There is, however, one crucial difference between giving presents to our friends, and offering worship to God: it is not for us to try to decide what will please God. God has already decided what kind of worship he wants. Worship that pleases him must be 'by the Spirit of God'.

'Well,' someone may say, 'if I'm going to worship God by his Spirit, then I'm not really doing anything. It's just God doing it for himself. But I want to please him by showing him what I can do.' But anyone who talks like this does not know God, because God doesn't want what we can do. He has already decided what he wants, and we must decide whether we are going to worship in his way. As the writer to the Hebrews says, 'By him therefore let us offer the sacrifice of praise to God continually' (Heb. 13:15). The word 'sacrifice' is used here because to worship by the Spirit of God involves self-denial. It is a *sacrifice* of praise.

One of the earliest worship services in the history of mankind is described in Genesis 4. And in it Cain decided that he would worship God by bringing an offering of the works of his own hands, while his brother Abel sacrificed some of his best lambs. But God wanted a sacrifice. So, 'The Lord had respect unto Abel and to his offering. But unto Cain and to his offering he had not respect' (vv.4–5).

Our aim in worship must be to please God, but the aim of worship is also to edify the soul of every person present. The key word here is *every* person. God is worshipped not just when we do certain things right, but when we are edified – that is, when our spirits are fed with his word, so that we reach out to him in repentance, gratitude and trust. He is glorified when we worship him with our understanding, not when we intone, parrot-fashion, words like, 'Majestic sweetness sits enthroned . . .' And he is not fully glorified if only some people are edified.

If we are rigid in our services, only a limited number of people will be blessed. If the order of worship is controlled by those who say, 'We've always done it this way,' then our worship may be irrelevant to new people. Why aren't we reaching out to the world? The answer may be that much of our worship is irrelevant. Why are some Anglo-Catholic churches dying? It's not just because of their liberal theology, but because their worship doesn't speak to people where they are. Only a minority of people today are interested in burning incense. And evangelical churches, with their rigid traditions, may also be failing to reach people. So often they are too busy arguing about minor points of order to get on with the task of evangelism.

A few years ago an academic study looked at revival in the Third World to see if the different revivals had any factors in common. Revivals in countries like Korea and in cities like Nairobi were studied. The conclusion was that they all had five things in common: an emphasis first, on prayer; second, on evangelism; third, on discipleship; fourth, on one church for all the people in the area; and fifth, on relevant worship.

Psychological studies tell us that a truly mature person is one who is adaptable. A refusal to accept the new and different may not indicate godliness or spiritual maturity, but fear. If our worship is to glorify God by being relevant, we must be willing to accept changes. There must be something for all types of people in our services. I believe that when revival comes, we will not find just one class of people in our churches, but all types and groups.

But I turn now to my third point, and that is doubtful worship. Philippians 3:3 says, 'We . . . rejoice in Christ Jesus, and have no confidence in the flesh.' I am talking here about worship which is 'fleshly', worship which is not dependent on God's Spirit. Such worship has three characteristics, the first of which is emotionalism. I can give you an example of this. I was once in Ohio, preaching for Dr Billy Ball. As we were driving down the Interstate 75 on our way back to the airport, we saw in the distance the old Union Station in Cincinnati, and I asked if we would have time to stop there. When I was a boy, my mother and I used to visit her parents in Illinois, and on the way we would always change trains in Cincinnati. We usually had an hour to spare, and I would walk all over this big station – the largest in the world at that time, and said to be the most beautiful. Today it's a shopping centre, because the railway industry in America has declined.

So we stopped, and I walked round the building with tears in my eyes. When I got back in the car I said, 'You'll never know what that did for me!' It had made me feel so good to be there. But the experience was emotional rather than spiritual.

And this sort of thing can happen in worship. We may like the building, or the sound of the organ, or the tunes of the hymns; we may feel good when we hear, 'A mighty fortress is our God', or – as we used to sing back in the hills of Kentucky – 'Tell Mother I'll be there in answer to her prayer'. But our 'good' feelings may be emotional only. May God grant us objectivity about ourselves, so that we can analyse why we are moved and ask, 'Is it truly of the Spirit, or just a natural human emotion?'

Another characteristic of fleshly, doubtful, worship is elitism, that is, worship that favours one cultural group and excludes others. For example, I love the pipe organ; in Westminster Chapel we have one of the finest organs in the country. But it is elitist to have only organ music in church.

A third characteristic is that it is entertainment worship, or worship that is for people's pleasure. Any worship which seeks to amuse or entertain people is only a performance and is to be despised. God wants us to use our talents, but for his glory. Godly singers and musicians lead us out to focus on God and worship him. When we find we are concentrating on the performer and praising him or her – that is fleshly, entertainment worship.

So, finally, I would like to describe dynamic worship. The word dynamic means fluid, moving. It is the opposite of static. Jonathan Edwards taught us that the task of every generation is to discover in which direction the sovereign Redeemer is moving, and then to move in that direction.

Dynamic worship is worship by the Spirit of God. And

we will know that the Spirit is present in our worship if these three things follow: an increase of faith, of fellowship and of freedom. We will leave after a service feeling we have faith to face a thousand worlds, with love in our hearts towards every single person in the church, and without our dreadful feelings of self-consciousness; for 'Where the Spirit of the Lord is, there is liberty' (2 Cor. 3:17).

A telling sign of true revival is that people are oblivious of everything but God. A couple of years ago I spoke to a man who had experienced revival in Africa. When I asked him to tell me about it, he said, 'Nobody was self-conscious. You were conscious only of God.' This means that we will not be intimidated by others. In his book, *Whatever Happened to Worship?* A. W. Tozer has this to say about Jesus' words: 'I tell you that, if these should hold their peace, the very stones would cry out' (Luke 19:40):

> Let me say two things here. First, I do not believe it is necessarily true that we are worshipping God when we are making a lot of racket. But not infrequently worship is audible.
>
> When Jesus came into Jerusalem, presenting himself as Messiah, there was a great multitude, and there was a great noise. Doubtless many who joined in the singing and the praise had never been able to sing in the right key. When you have a group of people singing anywhere, you know that some of them will not be in tune. But this is the point to their worship: they were united in praises to God.
>
> Second, I would warn those who are cultured, quiet, self-possessed, poised and sophisticated, that if they are embarrassed in church when some happy Christian says, 'Amen,' they may actually be in need of some spiritual enlightenment. The worshipping saints of God in the body of Christ have often been a little bit noisy.

In heaven there will be no sense of pride, or of fear; no looking over our shoulder. Heaven will be filled with praise to 'the Lamb that is on the throne'.

CHAPTER 2

EMPTY FORM OR TRUE WORSHIP

'For we are the circumcision, which worship God in the spirit, and rejoice in Christ Jesus, and have no confidence in the flesh.' (Philippians 3:3)

In chapter 1, I talked about suspect, or counterfeit, worship. Worship that is elitist or is reduced to the level of popular entertainment, worship that is emotional or aesthetic is worship in name only. It has the external form without the reality. What we long for is living worship. But how does this come about?

I think the principle to follow is to be found in Psalm 37:4, 'Delight thyself also in the Lord; and he shall give thee the desires of thine heart.' That is true for all of us, whoever we are or whatever we want. But when we delight ourselves in the Lord, some of our desires may wither away and be replaced by new ambitions. So it will not do to envisage a definite goal concerning the form our worship must take. We must first of all be sure that we are delighting ourselves in the Lord, and then see what God does.

I want to show you from Paul's words in Philippians 3:3 that worship which is 'by the Spirit of God' has three stages. First, the initiation of the Spirit; second, the impulse of the Spirit; and third, the inheritance of the Spirit.

So, firstly, the *initiation of the Spirit*. We must see here that God's elect – that is, those whom God has chosen – are a people of the Spirit. Now the Jews in Paul's day said that the people of God were those who had been circumcised. To this day, one is officially a Jew if one has a Jewish mother. Being a Jew is either inherited or initiated by circumcision. Many think it is the same with Christianity. They think that to be a Christian you must be born into a Christian home, or be baptised or attend a Christian church.

Not so, says Paul. God's elect are a people of the Spirit. In Romans 9:6b–7 Paul says, 'For they are not all Israel, which are of Israel. Neither, because they are the seed of Abraham, are they all children: but, In Isaac shall thy seed be called.' Ishmael, though a son of Abraham, was regarded as strictly of the flesh, whereas Isaac was the child of promise, and he was of the Spirit.

When Paul says, 'we are the circumcision', he means that God's people are circumcised in the heart: 'Circumcision is that of the heart' (Rom. 2:29). And this is a sovereign work of the Holy Spirit. Jesus said, 'It is the Spirit that quickeneth; the flesh profiteth nothing' (John 6:63). And Paul said in Romans 8:2: 'For the law of the Spirit of life in Christ Jesus hath made me free from the law of sin and death.' The only people who truly worship God are the people of the Spirit, who have had this operation of the Holy Spirit upon the foreskins of their hearts. Only the elect can worship God with spiritual worship. All others may say that they worship, but they are worshipping idols.

Our churches should not be places where the unregenerate come on Sundays because they 'like the worship'. Our churches ought to be places where the unregenerate feel uncomfortable because it is the Spirit who is important and who comes first. Our controlling principle must be obedience to the Spirit – no matter where he leads us.

And, further, worship which is initiated by the Spirit

24

is always of the Spirit, by the Spirit and in the Spirit. *Of the Spirit* refers to those who have been brought to the new birth; *by the Spirit* describes what these reborn people are able to do – they serve God under the impulse of the Spirit. And this is an internal thing, a matter of the heart. It may be expressed externally, but it is immaterial whether this be by tambourine, guitar or a pipe organ.

Lastly, worship which is in the Spirit is brought about when, under the impulse of the Spirit, God's people are taken a step further, so that they begin to adore the triune God on a level which is different from anything they have ever experienced before, a level which transcends elitist or emotional or entertainment worship. And this is not something which can be worked up by hand-clapping, or forcing your hand into the air, or by any self-induced enthusiasm.

This leads me to my second point: *the impulse of the Spirit*. As I have said, the Greek of Philippians 3:3 reads 'who worship by the impulse of the Spirit'. Now this is a very important concept, yet I have a suspicion that we largely do not know anything about it. You have probably heard it said that if the Holy Spirit left a church, ninety per cent of the work of that church would go right on as if nothing had happened. And I suspect that this would also be true with reference to church worship.

We say, 'Oh, but we like it this way. We have always done it this way.' But where does the impulse of the Spirit come in?

In true worship the people of the Spirit are enabled by the Spirit to participate in the worship which God feels for himself. For God loves himself – and if we don't like that fact, it is because a God of glory is offensive to our fleshly human nature. God does everything for his own glory, and 'Worketh all things after the counsel of his own will' (Eph. 1:11b). And everything in all creation was designed for the worship of God. If you don't like the idea of worshipping God, if you want to go your own way, and do your own thing, then you are going against the very reason God made you. God's entire plan of salvation is designed to bring us to the place where we worship God: 'Let all the angels of God worship him' (Heb. 1:6); 'Let every thing that hath breath [whether it be fish or fowl, mammal or flower] praise the Lord' (Ps. 150:6); 'The heavens declare the glory of God' (Ps. 19:1). Under the impulse of the Spirit we are brought to worship God as God worships himself. And therefore, if we are worshipping under the impulse of the Spirit, we ourselves are not doing anything. In John 6:63 we read: 'The flesh profiteth nothing.' Paul continues Philippians 3:3 with the words, '. . . have no confidence in the flesh'.

As long as we think that we are doing something – that there is something in us, whether it be talents, or our efforts, or our self-denial, or an idea that we can make promises to God – and as long as we call this worship, then we need to be reminded that we are taking our cue from the flesh. We need to be advised that this is mainly self-love, not the worship of God.

We must also understand that worship by the impulse of the Spirit is done by degrees. And some may experience a higher degree of this impulse than others. As we have seen, the principle here is that the greater the measure of the Spirit, the less we will be conscious of those around us, and the more we will become aware of God. Should the Spirit increase in us in great measure (what a blessed thought!), the result might be total unconsciousness. John on the Isle of Patmos said, 'When I saw him, I fell at his feet as dead' (Rev. 1:17). The prophet Ezekiel said, 'And, behold, the glory of the God of Israel was there . . . in the plain . . . And it came to pass . . . that I fell upon my face' (Ezek. 8:4; 9:8).

The Cane Ridge Revival in America has been called America's Second Great Awakening. It is not so well known in this country because there were no great preachers like Edwards or Whitefield. Instead there were provincial preachers. One Sunday morning in July 1800, fifteen thousand people came under the influence of the Spirit, and eye-witnesses said that that Sunday morning service continued without a break until midday on the following Wednesday.

People were praising God and worshipping and as many as five hundred at a time were unconscious on the ground. They were thought to be dead. Their pulses were checked and were found to be down to only two or three beats a minute. And yet the people came out of it with a great sense of God.

That's having a degree of the Spirit!

There is a famous story from the Welsh Revival. A man came home from the coal mines to find that for the fifth or sixth night in succession his wife had gone down to the church where the revival was taking place, and had not prepared his supper. He was so mad that he went down to the revival with the express purpose of busting it wide open and pulling his wife out.

But when he got to the church it was so crowded that he couldn't get in. There were even people standing outside. He tried to work his way through, and the next thing he knew, he was on his knees in front of the altar, with his hands in the air, praying.

That measure of the Spirit has happened in Church history, but this generation, and that includes those in the charismatic movement, I fear know little or nothing about it.

I would like to give a two-fold warning here. First, never think that an outpouring of the Holy Spirit will convince everybody. And, second, never think that those who are affected will be affected equally.

Perhaps the key here is the sovereignty of the Spirit. It is one thing to believe in the sovereignty of the Spirit with reference to salvation, but another to believe in his sovereignty with reference to worship. You may be affected, but the person next to you may be totally unmoved. You may be thinking, 'Oh, Lord, this is marvellous,' and then you may wonder what is going on in your neighbour's mind. What a pity if you were to grieve or quench the Spirit, or cast aside his impulse, because you were influenced by what another might or might not be thinking.

You may say, 'Surely, if the Spirit comes in power, I won't be concerned with anybody else.' But it's not always as simple as that. Jesus said, 'He that is faithful in that which is least is faithful also in much' (Luke 16:10). I used to think that if revival ever came to my own church, Westminster Chapel, I would then be able to get away with calling people forward. And people would say, 'There's such power here, they're coming forward in droves.'

But then I realised that I had to call people forward in a non-revival atmosphere, painful though that might be. And so with each individual. You may want that great power, but, 'He that is faithful in that which is least is faithful also in much.' When you are in a church service, God could pass by the person next to you for the moment, but if you go by what is happening to him, and so quench the Spirit in yourself, you will miss the blessing, which may well come to your neighbour later. In fact, God may slay the person next to you later and never come back to you at all because looking over your shoulder all the time shows that you care more about what people think than what God thinks.

The warning is that it is possible to be present where the Spirit is working in great power, and yet feel nothing yourself. Never say, 'I would know an authentic work of the Spirit,' for that kind of pride only grieves the Spirit. God could come in great power and people could be affected but you might not feel a thing. You might even laugh and say, 'Look at them – silly people!'

When Jesus raised Lazarus from the dead, you would think everybody would have believed in him. But they didn't. We read that, 'Many of the Jews which came to Mary, and had seen the things which Jesus did, believed on him. But some of them went their ways to the Pharisees, and told them what things Jesus had done' (John 11:45–46).

I used to say to myself, 'If only revival would come, all those who oppose my ministry would see that I really am a man of God.' But Luke 16:10 says, 'He that is unjust in the least is unjust also in much.' No great movement of the Spirit has ever convinced everybody. Have you any idea of the kind of critics Evan Roberts had in his day? Or of the number who criticised Whitefield and Edwards?

I think we would all agree that Stephen, the first deacon, preached with unction. And you couldn't have suggested to the Pharisee, Saul of Tarsus, that he would not recognise the work of God. He considered himself an authority on it. But Saul of Tarsus heard Stephen preach, and was unimpressed. There was Stephen, with his face shining like an angel, saying, 'Behold, I see the heavens opened, and the Son of man standing on the right hand of God' (Acts 7:56). Yet Saul consented to Stephen's death.

Never think that you are so in touch with God that nothing could come to your church without your knowing it first. One of the errors of some charismatic Christians is that they see the Spirit as a warm blanket that falls on everybody so that everybody feels the same thing. But the outpouring of the sovereign Spirit is essentially upon individuals. Each worshipper is responsible to God alone. The task for each of us is to say, 'God, it's you I worship.' God is willing to pour out his Spirit on those who look to him only. Jesus said, 'How can ye believe, which receive honour one of another, and seek not the honour that cometh from God only?' (John 5:44).

So now I move on to *the inheritance of the Spirit*. This is when the Holy Spirit is utterly himself in us. When someone comes into our house we say, 'Do make yourself at home.' If you really want the Spirit to be at home in you – to be himself in you – you must open your heart directly to him and say, 'Lord, I do love you, and I will do what you say.'

Complete obedience to the Spirit at home within us is the key to true worship, either when we are by ourselves, or with other Christians at church. The worship we experience when we are alone ought to be multiplied a hundred times when we come to the church worship service, otherwise we are godly on weekdays and hypocrites on Sundays. If we say that we are loving and seeking God, but quench the Spirit when we meet together with other Christians, what kind of love is that?

Do we want revival – the culmination of true worship? It's easier to pray twice a day for it than obey God when he says, 'But here's what I want you to do.' We may admire Evan Roberts who said in agony, 'Lord, bend me.' But God is asking all of us to say, 'Bend me' and mean it, regardless of the cost.

CHAPTER 3

HONOURING THE SPIRIT

'For we . . . worship God in the spirit, and rejoice in Christ Jesus, and have no confidence in the flesh.' (Philippians 3:3)

If you were to ask people to describe to you their idea of a perfect service of worship, I suspect that many, or most, would start by describing the external organisation and shape of the service. Should there be banjos or violins or organ music? Should there be a hymnal or choruses? What about the prayer book?

However, as I hope I have shown, I am not primarily concerned with that, although it would be interesting to see what forms of worship would emerge in a church fully given over to the leading of the Spirit.

We have seen that God is a God of glory. He loves himself and 'worketh all things after the counsel of his own will' (Eph. 1:11). He knows how he wants to be worshipped: it won't do for us, in our desire for creativity, just to come up with a way we *think* honours him. We must be controlled by the Spirit from start to finish.

As Paul says, we must 'have no confidence in the flesh' (Phil. 3:3b). If we begin with the form of worship, we are beginning with the flesh, because at once we are superimposing a cultural norm on the worship. But how will we ever know what is truly spiritual? How will we avoid

31

'having a form of godliness, but denying the power thereof' (2 Tim. 3:5)?

When I look at Philippians 3:3 the immediate question that I ask is, 'What does it mean to bring the Spirit in to our worship?' When Paul says, 'We . . . worship in the Spirit,' what does that mean?

In this chapter I want to look at three possible approaches to the Holy Spirit. The first possibility is hiring him, that is, engaging his services for temporary use. The second is hindering the Spirit – Paul calls it 'grieving' him. And the third is honouring him.

First, hiring him. How do we hire the Spirit? The word 'hire' means to engage the services of a person or a place or a thing. I think that many of us in our worship are like someone without a car who wants to take a trip from London to Brighton, and wonders how to get there – by train, perhaps, or by hiring a car.

Suppose we decide to hire a car, a Ford Cortina perhaps. We walk up to it and say, 'Hmm – looks like a nice car.' But do we then say, 'How are you doing, Ford Cortina? Where would you like to go today?' Of course we don't! We make it do what we want, because it has no will of its own. And many of us do just this with the Holy Spirit. We treat him as if he has no will of his own. We think of him as standing idly by, wanting to be used, like a car waiting to be hired.

We decide what we want to include in our services and what our aim is to be and then tell the Holy Spirit to take us there. When we hire the Spirit in this way we manipulate him to serve our own ends, and that is a great abuse.

Another abuse of the Spirit that results from hiring him, is to try and work him up to go our way. I have been in places where there has been fifteen or twenty minutes of clapping and tambourine playing to get the service going. Sometimes you almost feel as though you are watching American cheer leaders before a football game.

We have an instance of this kind of approach in 1 Kings

18, when Elijah challenged the prophets of Baal to meet him on Mount Carmel and see who was worshipping the true God.

> And Elijah said unto the prophets of Baal, Choose you one bullock for yourselves, and dress it first; for ye are many; and call on the name of your gods, but put no fire under. And they took the bullock which was given them, and they dressed it, and called on the name of Baal from morning even until noon, saying, O Baal, hear us. But there was no voice, nor any that answered. And they leaped upon the altar which was made. And it came to pass at noon, that Elijah mocked them, and said, Cry aloud: for he is a god; either he is talking, or he is pursuing, or he is in a journey, or peradventure he sleepeth, and must be awaked.
> And they cried aloud, and cut themselves after their manner with knives and lancets, till the blood gushed out upon them. (1 Kings 18:25–28)

This sort of behaviour is merely of the flesh. People suppose that noise proves the presence of the Spirit. I have already quoted the remark by A. W. Tozer that when the Spirit is powerfully present there is often a lot of noise, and I agree with that. But Tozer himself went on to say that noise does not always prove that the Spirit is there.

I come next to hindering the Spirit. One way of doing this is to hem him around with our own preconceived ideas and prejudices. This happens when we come to worship after having already decided on the form the worship should take. Nothing quenches the Spirit like prejudice of this sort. And one problem is that so often we don't recognise it in ourselves. Whether our prejudices are racial or cultural, intellectual or political, we feel good about them, and think they must be right. And because we feel so good, because we feel at home with our prejudices, we think that what we are feeling comes from the Holy Spirit. It is a subtle trap. And as a result many people never have any idea of what God can do in them and through them.

It is wrong to claim that a particular form, which was once truly used by the Spirit, must therefore always be the only valid form. The Welsh Revival, for example, was often criticised because its emphasis was on singing and there was so little preaching, for in the days of Whitefield preaching had the priority.

The question for us is: where is God now? The Spirit is not for hire. We don't have to work anything up, for the Spirit has a will of his own and he alone knows what the God of glory desires. Our task is to listen to him and find out what this is.

Another way of hindering the Spirit is to shut him out by our hardness of heart. Sometimes we have a proud, independent attitude which the Spirit just cannot penetrate.

You may say, 'But God is sovereign. He can work by irresistible grace.' It is true that this applies sooner or later in the effectual calling of the elect, but it does not apply to the living of the Christian life. The doctrine of sanctification is *not* worked out by irresistible grace. If our sanctification happened automatically, through irresistible grace, we would not need the New Testament, or the urgings of Paul.

The fact is, that the Holy Spirit, although he works effectually in bringing people to saving faith, is easily grieved and hindered, and when we come to church with hard hearts, nothing will happen. Maybe we do not physically have our arms folded, but we do in spirit; maybe we are not outwardly stiff-necked, but we are in spirit. We justify our pride, and our failure to love, and think all this has nothing to do with worship. But remember that Jesus said, 'Ye are they which justify yourselves before men; but God knoweth your hearts: for that which is highly esteemed among men is abomination in the sight of God' (Luke 16:15).

A third way of hindering the Spirit is by intentionally pushing him away. In these cases Satan takes over to make sure that the Spirit is diverted. For Satan is threatened by truly spiritual worship, and he will do anything to hold us back. One of his methods is to plant people in the congregation whose very presence will divert and hinder the Spirit. And these people know what they are doing. At Satan's instigation people will sometimes call out during the service. There may be a drunk or a demon-possessed person in the congregation. In a congregation of many people even one individual can hinder the work of the Spirit. Not to believe that is to misunderstand how the Spirit acts.

One summer I was preaching in a church in the Florida Keys, and as I began to talk about the blood of Jesus, someone who had been brought along specially to hear me preach began to call out to me in a very strange voice. It got worse and worse until finally I told everybody to bow their heads. We sang a chorus while the person was removed, and at once the atmosphere changed. You could feel the presence of God, and by the time we finished the service some had even forgotten what had happened.

We are engaged in warfare against Satan. Ephesians 6:12 says, 'For we wrestle not against flesh and blood, but against principalities, against powers, against the rulers of the darkness of this world.' All of us need to be aware of Satan's ways of hindering the Spirit during worship, and I will be looking at this in more detail in Chapter 15.

How, then, do we *honour* the Spirit? We must never forget that he is a person: the third person of the Trinity, and we must respect him. We must learn, first of all, to respect his sensitivity. Many people do not realise that he is easily grieved, easily offended and quenched. I do not mean that he is sensitive in the way proud people are sensitive. There are many people to whom you hardly dare speak because you are always putting your foot in it and injuring their feelings in some way. No, the Holy Spirit is sensitive, if only because he is so utterly pure and holy. He cannot be free to work where there is sin and there is sin wherever people are depending on themselves instead of coming to Jesus for forgiveness and power to live their lives.

But we must respect not only the Spirit's sensitivity, but also his impartiality. He is 'no respecter of persons' (Acts 10:34). He cannot be bought, he cannot be paid off, he cannot be influenced. You can't make any secret deals with him. Many people seem to think – often without even realising they think it – that if they have been a Christian, perhaps a deacon or a preacher, for a very long time, then they can come to an understanding with the Spirit, and be granted a special indemnity on the basis of past service.

But you can be a Christian for thirty years and find he is no longer working in you because you have suddenly grieved him, while someone who has been converted less than six months can have the Spirit in great power and be much used by God. You may think that this is not fair on a Christian who has 'borne the burden and heat of the day' (Matt. 20:12). But Jesus said, 'So the last shall be first, and the first last' (Matt. 20:16). The Spirit is no respecter of persons.

We must also respect and obey the Spirit's impulse. That is, as we saw in Chapter 2, we must let him be himself in us. This means that we must let him be himself in others, too. We ought not to judge the style of another person's worship.

Some of our fathers were given great discernment, and could recognise the presence of the Spirit. The man whom God used more than any other in the Welsh Revival was Evan Roberts. But for a year or two before the Revival began, many people were worried about Evan

Roberts. They thought there was something strange about him.

But then a man arrived who had been present fifty years before, at the Welsh Revival of 1859, and who knew something of the ways of the Spirit. And when he heard that people were criticising Evan Roberts, he said, 'Don't put a hand on that boy. God is dealing with him.' He could recognise the work of the Spirit.

One of my childhood memories is of a two-week meeting in my church in Ashland. On the last night they brought in one of the greatest preachers I had ever heard. And the place was packed, with everybody waiting expectantly to hear the sermon. But when he walked into the pulpit the man just said, 'God is here.' Then he began singing the chorus:

How wonderful, wonderful Jesus is to me,
Counsellor, Prince of Peace, mighty God is he.

Everybody began to sing with him and God's power was present there. Within about ten minutes fifty or sixty people must have spontaneously stood up and walked down to kneel at the front. Yet that man didn't even preach. Most preachers want to deliver a sermon which they have worked hard to prepare, because, after all, people have come to hear them speak. But this man recognised the Spirit, and knew that it was far more important to release him than to preach.

This brings me to the final point: we honour the Spirit by releasing him. Jesus said, 'He that believeth on me, as the scripture hath said, out of his belly shall flow rivers of living water' (John 7:38). Many of us think only in terms of the Spirit coming down, but he can flow out from a well deep within us.

How do we release the Spirit, both in ourselves and in others? In ourselves it will happen when we keep peace in our hearts with everybody we know. Sometimes we play games with ourselves, and pretend we are at peace and that all is fine. It is like someone who loses his temper and then says, 'I'm not mad.' We can justify ourselves until we are a hundred, but the Spirit will never be himself in us as long as we are unforgiving or judgmental, prejudiced, or speaking evil of anyone. He will not be himself in us as long as we are preoccupied with what others are going to think of what we do. It may mean apologising to someone, or it may be a little thing like raising your hand in worship. But obeying his impulse is all part of honouring the Spirit and releasing him in ourselves.

And we can release the Spirit in others when we relinquish our control over other people. We can refuse to let another person be afraid of us, or admire us too much. (We never do anyone a favour by letting them admire us too much, for sooner or later we will disappoint them.) Or we can refuse to let other people feel under an obligation to us. The flesh, you see, always wants to control. Some ministers want to control their congregations, and some leaders of house churches want to be in control. But the Spirit gives liberty and through him we must release others to be themselves – to think for themselves. There may be people who are in bondage just because they are afraid of us, but we can help them. And when we do, the Spirit will be released to be himself in all of us.

If you are wondering what on earth all this has got to do with the worship service, then I would repeat that worship is not primarily a matter of outward form. It is a matter of the heart. So what we have been talking about has everything to do with the worship service. What happens in our personal lives cannot be divorced from the Spirit's work in public worship.

I was named after my father's favourite preacher – R. T. Williams. I grew up hearing about him, and he must have been a remarkable man. When old Dr Williams spoke to young men whom he had just ordained into the ministry, he always said the same thing: 'Young men, honour the blood. And honour the Holy Ghost.'

In the days of revival those whom God used were able to recognise the Spirit and honour him. They would not get in his way – even if it meant not preaching.

Suppose five hundred people, all of whom possessed the ungrieved Spirit – or rather, all of whom were possessed by the ungrieved Spirit – were to come together to worship? I would love to know what would happen. It could be a spontaneous combustion such as no nuclear explosion has ever produced!

CHAPTER 4

FELLOWSHIP

'And they continued stedfastly . . . in fellowship . . .' (Acts
2:42)

It is sometimes said that British people are characterised
by the 'stiff upper lip'. This means that when someone
hurts you, you never show it, so that the person who hurts
you doesn't even know.

Often when we grieve the Holy Spirit we only realise
weeks or even months later that we have hurt him. I
define spirituality as the ability to close the time gap
between the moment we sin and the moment we realise
that we have sinned and therefore grieved the Holy
Spirit. Some of us are so proud and self-willed, and so
sure that we are right, that it takes us years before we
realise what we have done. But we can learn to bring the
time gap down to seconds, and even catch ourselves
before we sin and so avoid grieving the Spirit.

In the last chapter I talked about grieving the Spirit,
and I want to continue with this, looking particularly at
the subject of fellowship, and the bitterness of spirit that
destroys fellowship.

You may say, 'What on earth has that to do with worship?' And I would reply: 'Everything. You just cannot
worship in the Spirit if you are out of sorts with your fel-
low Christians.'

40

When Paul said in Ephesians 4:30, 'And grieve not the holy Spirit of God, whereby ye are sealed unto the day of redemption,' the very next thing he said was, 'Let all bitterness, and wrath, and anger, and clamour, and evil speaking, be put away from you, with all malice. And be ye kind one to another, tenderhearted, forgiving one another, even as God for Christ's sake hath forgiven you' (vv.31–32).

You may think, 'Well, God understands that I have always had a problem with forgiving people.' But you don't have any more of a problem than anybody else: 'There hath no temptation taken you but such as is common to man' (1 Cor. 10:13). You may justify your hurt, but in doing so you grieve the Holy Spirit.

Now bitterness can be directed towards God, towards others or towards ourselves. We are bitter towards God if we get angry about what he has allowed to happen. This prevents us worshipping by the Spirit, because we can't worship God very well if we are angry with him.

Bitterness towards others comes when we are hurt over what they have done to us, and we feel bitterness towards ourselves when we cannot forgive ourselves for what we have done. This shows that we have not accepted the promise, 'If we confess our sins, he is faithful and just to forgive us our sins and to cleanse us from all unrighteousness' (1 John 1:9). We are trying to dictate to God when we refuse to forgive ourselves when he has forgiven us.

I know what it is to be bitter – and to be bitter for a long time. And I know what it is to justify myself all the time by saying, 'God understands.' He does. But all the time we are being bitter, the Holy Spirit is being grieved, and we will not know his impulse within us.

A verse which people often prefer to ignore in this connection is 1 Peter 3:7: 'Likewise, ye husbands, dwell with them [your wives] according to knowledge, giving honour unto the wife, as to the weaker vessel, and as being heirs together of the grace of life; *that your prayers be not hindered'* (italics mine).

It is so easy for a husband to get very annoyed with his wife. She may be late doing something, perhaps, or she may get something wrong, and he feels upset. He decides to read his Bible and pray for a while, and it doesn't seem to occur to him that his prayers may be hindered. He simply says to himself, 'I'm going to pray. Here I go: Heavenly Father, I'm just going to trust you. I'm mad at her! But you understand, and you'll give me a verse here today. Oh, here's one. No, I don't like that verse, I think I'll read this one . . .' And all the time the Spirit is grieved.

If a husband is sensitive, he will know that he will not be able to get on with praying until he has got things right again with his wife. I remind you of the statement made by a psychologist from UCLA. He said that after twenty-five years of marriage counselling, he had come to the conclusion that in most all cases of trouble it is the man's fault.

1 Peter 3:7 states a general principle; it applies, of course, to the wife, and it also operates in the office, at university, or school. It prohibits any bitterness towards your boss, a colleague or school friend.

You may be thinking by now, 'Well, this is pretty difficult.'

It is. That is precisely why the people whom God has used in history are signally rare. But it needn't be that way. If only the congregations in our churches lived like this seven days a week, then, when they came together to sing the hymns and participate in the Lord's Supper, the worship wouldn't be a mockery.

The earliest record of any pattern of worship is found in Acts 2:42, where we have a description of what immediately followed the baptism of the three thousand people who were saved after Peter's sermon on the day of Pentecost. It says, 'And they continued stedfastly in the apostles' doctrine and fellowship, and in breaking of bread and in prayers.'

From this verse you can see the importance of fellowship in the worshipping life of the early Church. If fellowship is not present, worship ceases. But what constituted fellowship? The answer is that two things were shared: a common faith and a common enemy. Three thousand people may seem like a good number, but compared to the hundreds of thousands who were in Jerusalem at that time, it was a very small minority.

These three thousand all believed in the resurrection of Jesus. They had all just been baptised and were full of the Holy Spirit. And they were hated by the religious and secular leaders. But, in face of this opposition, they had each other.

We know that the world has nothing in common with us and we come together to be with people who share what we believe. In the early Church no one was at odds with anyone else at first. There was such power present that they were actually detached from their worldly possessions (Acts 2:44).

The world looked on and sensed that something special was happening. Acts 5:13 says, 'And of the rest durst no man join himself to them.' The non-Christian Jews were in awe of Christians at the time, and they could not join them unless the Holy Spirit brought them in.

That is what is needed today, but it is impossible when people in church avoid each other. Jonathan Edwards said that Satan had training in the greatest university that ever was – in the heaven of heavens. And oh how the devil knows how to hinder the moving of the Spirit! It is not enough to sing hymns or to listen to preaching or be sound in doctrine. If we want New Testament worship, then we must see that fellowship is a vital and necessary ingredient of the worship.

We also see from Acts 2:42 that in the early Christian community there was preaching ('the apostles' doctrine'), breaking of bread and prayer and I will look at these in following chapters. But it is interesting to note here the order of these things: doctrine, fellowship and then the Lord's Supper and prayer. This indicates that we have no right to partake of the Lord's Supper when we are out of fellowship with others who are present. We will not be able to worship God if we have not made an attempt to put things right. As we have seen, we grieve the Holy Spirit if it is within our power to release another person by what we say and yet we do nothing about it.

I know there are times when we just can't sort things out. We can talk to some people for hours and get nowhere with them. But at least we have followed the New Testament pattern and tried. Paul said, 'If it be possible, as much as lieth in you, live peaceably with all men' (Rom. 12:18) – our heavenly Father loves all of us equally. However, what is important is that we ourselves should not be harbouring animosity and bitterness.

Acts 2 concludes with this lovely description of the early Church: 'And they continuing daily with one accord in the temple, and breaking bread from house to house, did eat their meat with gladness and singleness of heart, praising God, and having favour with all the people. And the Lord added to the church daily such as should be saved.'

When in our worship there is fellowship and love, then the joy we experience flows out into a life of praise and witness.

CHAPTER 5

WORSHIP, PREACHING AND THE
PREACHER

'And they continued stedfastly in the apostles' doctrine . . .'
(Acts 2:42)

In my opinion, the call to preach is the highest calling in
the world and the highest honour that God can bestow
on any man. There is a sense in which preaching is the
most tangible link between men and the triune God.

But it is also the greatest responsibility that there is.
Charles Spurgeon used to give this advice to any who
were undecided about whether or not they ought to
become ministers of the gospel: 'If you can do anything
else, do it.' He meant that if you can succeed at anything
else, then you are not called to preach. On the other
hand, a minister who *is* called would be like a fish out of
water anywhere except in the pulpit.

Let me remind you of our definition of worship: it is
the response to, and/or preparation for, the preached
word. This definition obviously makes preaching central
to worship. This was one of the discoveries made way
back in the sixteenth century. The rediscovery of justification by faith was only one part of the Great Reformation.
There was also a rediscovery of preaching, for in the
Middle Ages the emphasis had been on the sacraments.

It is quite wrong to refer to the singing – both hymns

and choruses – as though they alone comprise the worship. This is easy to do. We tend to think of the morning and evening service as if it is divided into two parts: first the worship, and then the preaching.

We must, of course, never underestimate the importance and the impact of singing, and I will be devoting two chapters to music and singing. There is music and singing in heaven. God can speak through the hymns, and we worship him in them. Our English hymnody is unexcelled in the world, and I spend considerable time choosing the hymns in order to get them exactly right. But the thrust and pinnacle of worship lies in the preaching. In the book of Acts, which is the earliest historical account of the Church, the emphasis is not on singing. It is not even on the Lord's Supper. On every page – almost, it seems, on every other line – the emphasis is on preaching.

In this chapter I want us to see not only the centrality of preaching in worship, but that preaching should itself *be* worship. Even as the preacher speaks, we should all be worshipping. How can this be true? Well, simply because preaching is God's chosen way to save people. Paul says in 1 Corinthians 1:21: 'For after that in the wisdom of God the world by wisdom knew not God, it pleased God by the foolishness of preaching to save them that believe.' It doesn't say, 'By foolish preaching,' although there is enough of that around. It says, 'by the foolishness of preaching'. And when Paul wrote to Titus he said that God 'hath in due times manifested his word through preaching' (Tit. 1:3).

Here is a very simple definition of preaching: 'preaching is God's word reaching man through human personality.' The chief thing about preaching is that it must bring a real sense of God, not just of the word of God, but of God himself. And we will never worship unless that happens. So Paul could say in 1 Corinthians 2:4–5: 'And my speech and my preaching was not with enticing words of man's wisdom, but in demonstration of the Spirit and of power. That your faith should not stand in the wisdom of men, but in the power of God.'

God uses ordinary men, and the preacher's personality actually becomes the very instrument of God. But for this to happen, the preacher must be called, prepared, uncontrived and unafraid. If he does not have these characteristics, there will be bad preaching.

It is possible to have good speaking, but bad preaching. Notice that in the verse I have just quoted, Paul refers to 'my speech and my preaching'. He distinguished between the two. It is possible to be only speaking and not actually preaching, even though it may be called preaching.

And it is also possible for there to be bad speaking but good preaching. In 2 Corinthians 10:10, Paul refers to the way some of the people at Corinth talked about him. We read, 'For his letters, say they, are weighty and powerful; but his bodily presence is weak, and his speech contemptible.' They thought his speaking amounted to nothing. Imagine anyone saying that about the great apostle Paul!

For worship to take place through preaching, there must be soundness, urgency and relevance. The preaching must also be gripping and effectual. We can visualise preaching as a pyramid with five layers representing soundness, relevance, urgency, the ability to grip the hearer, and, at the pinnacle, an effectual quality. Preaching which is 'by the impulse of the Spirit' must have all these five elements. However, preaching can display the first four of these qualities without the Holy Spirit. But preaching will only be effectual if the Holy Spirit is present.

Sound preaching is preaching that is theologically and biblically correct. Paul said, 'I determined not to know any thing among you, save Jesus Christ, and him crucified' (1 Cor. 2:2). This was at the heart of all his preaching. And all theology, rightly understood, comes down to that: 'Jesus Christ and him crucified'. The importance of sound teaching must never be underestimated, and a preacher's exegesis – his interpretation of Scripture – *must* be correct.

The second level, relevance, means that the preaching

ought to touch the lives of the listeners. Look how Paul puts it: 'My speech and my preaching was not with enticing words of man's wisdom, but in demonstration of the Spirit and of power. That your faith should not stand in the wisdom of men, but in the power of God' (1 Cor. 2:4–5). Paul was determined that his preaching should relate to the faith of his hearers.

But that is not enough. There must be urgency. Paul said, 'I was with you in weakness, and in fear, and in much trembling' (1 Cor. 2:3). This was because of the urgency he felt. The preacher must long for the hearers to understand what is meant and why it *must* be believed.

And the preaching must also be gripping, that is, it must stir the heart of the listeners. It must break through defensive barriers.

But preaching which is gripping may still be ineffectual. In Acts 24:24–25 we read, 'And after certain days, when Felix came with his wife Drusilla, which was a Jewess, he sent for Paul, and heard him concerning the faith in Christ. And as he reasoned of righteousness, temperance, and judgment to come, Felix trembled, and answered, Go thy way for this time; when I have a convenient season, I will call for thee.'

Where Felix was concerned, Paul's preaching was not effectual. And this can be the case not only when the preaching is to non-Christians but when it is to Christians in the Sunday services. I am quite sure that many people are often gripped by the Sunday sermon, but they just think, 'I'm not ready to do that yet.' Like Felix, they say, 'When I have a convenient season, I will call for thee.'

When preaching is effectual, worship takes place, for then the preaching is not with the words of man's wisdom, but by the demonstration of the Spirit and of power, so that the listener is caught up into the heavenlies and loses sight of everything but God's voice. Some people may even start to laugh or to cry while the preacher is speaking, but the intercourse between God and man goes on unbroken. And this is what every preacher longs for.

Effectual preaching leads to repentance, which means 'a change of mind leading to a change of life'. For one person this may mean a one hundred and eighty degree turn, whereas for another, who is already walking in the light, it may lead to only a slight shift in direction.

Sometimes only one person in a congregation responds with repentance, or maybe hundreds will: and this is a time of great rejoicing indeed. Then the preacher and the listener are in the Spirit, and a surge of heaven – a wave of glory – sweeps over the congregation, so that everyone knows that everyone else feels the same way. This is what we mean when we speak of unction.

The preacher may be aware of three things while he is preaching. Sometimes he may feel nothing at all – yet the congregation feels the presence of God's Spirit. The preacher may be like Moses, who did not know 'the glory of his countenance' (2 Cor. 3:7b). I think there are few things more encouraging (it has happened to me more than once) than to leave the pulpit feeling an utter failure, only to find that after all someone was spoken to or converted.

But sometimes when I am preaching I enjoy myself considerably – only to come down from the pulpit and find I was the only one!

Thirdly, and joy of joys, is when the preacher and congregation together are filled with a sense of the presence of God: where there is the unction I have just referred to. This is a weighty responsibility for the minister because up to a point he can control this surge of the Spirit. It is a great mystery, but it is absolutely true. This is another reason why Paul said, 'I was with you in weakness, and in fear, and in much trembling' (1 Cor. 2:3).

I can tell you these things because I have learned them by sad and happy experience. I know what it is to have the Spirit working in great power in me – I can feel it when I am preaching. And when that happens, I know I must do two things. First, I must follow the impulse of the Spirit, and second, I must not try to control what is happening or intrude myself in any way. For at these times there is a warfare going on in the pulpit, and Satan will do anything he can to divert me. He may, for example, cause me to hear a noise, or to notice a particular look on someone's face. Or the temptation may come to say something I ought not to say. If I give in, the surge of the Spirit will suddenly diminish. I have quenched him myself, and have kept my congregation bound, instead of releasing them.

Finally, to be honest about what can happen when someone is preaching, I ought to include a fourth possibility: the preacher may feel nothing and the people may feel nothing! But I hope that doesn't happen too often.

Preaching which is by the Spirit of God occurs when the Spirit works through the preacher without any hindrance. For this to happen there must first be no self-righteousness in the preacher. The moment he puts himself up on a pedestal as if he thinks he is better than his congregation, he will lose all his effectiveness.

Second, he must not preach at anyone directly, because this is always counter-productive. One of the temptations a minister faces is to preach in a special way if he knows a certain person is in the congregation. There's not a minister in the world who doesn't know what I am talking about here. But nine times out of ten when I have given into this temptation and planned a special sermon, the person I thought would be present has not turned up! I think this is due to the mercy of God, because I know that every time I do a thing like that I am ineffective. One can be effective only when one is oblivious of who is present. Only then will the listeners be set free.

Third, the preacher must not inject any private opinions into his sermons.

Fourth, he must bring no grudges whatever into the pulpit. It is only too possible to preach while harbouring grievances — I know, I've done it myself — but at those times I've not had any anointing.

Finally, the preacher must say what he knows the Spirit wants him to say, even if it is not going to be popular.

But all this means that the minister's life must be given over to God twenty-four hours a day, seven days a week. The greatest folly of any preacher is to think that he can become the vehicle of God just by stepping into the pulpit; this can only come about as the outflow of a lifestyle. Every pastor and clergyman should ask himself: 'Do I please God? What if the people really did follow me and every member of my church were just like me? What if they prayed no more than I did? What if they forgave those who hurt them only to the extent that I forgave?' It is a sobering thought.

My first five years at Westminster Chapel were pleasant and uneventful. But then a great change came over my ministry. What changed it all was something which happened to me in the manse at midnight on April 14th 1982. Arthur Blessitt had spent the evening with us and we were on our knees praying. I asked Arthur to pray that I would have unction. I reckoned that if I could get such a man as Arthur to pray for me, God would really answer the prayer. But Arthur just said to me, 'You know, unction is not something that only comes when you walk into a pulpit: it's what flows out of a life.'

And Arthur thought he had hurt me and had lost a friend by saying that. But it was what I most needed to hear. I saw that night that something had to happen to me. A fundamental change was required in me. And I died a thousand deaths. I had wanted something to happen when I went into the pulpit, but God showed me it wasn't going to be that way. I had to change. And I have never been the same since.

However, suppose that all I have described in this chapter has happened. Suppose the word has gone out in the power of the Spirit from a preacher who is living in the power of the Spirit, it is possible that those listening may still not be converted or led into worship. This is because a very great responsibility also lies with the congregation. And this is what I want to turn to in the next chapter.

CHAPTER 6

WORSHIP AND LISTENING

'Faith comes by hearing, and hearing by the word of God.'
(Romans 10:17)

What can be more important than correct listening? We only worship God to the degree that we hear him speak. This is why there are injunctions throughout Scripture about hearing and listening. Jesus would frequently end a parable with the words, 'He that hath ears to hear, let him hear.' The psalmist said, 'Today if ye will hear his voice, harden not your heart, as in the provocation' (Ps. 95:7–8). This was echoed in Hebrews 3:8. There is also the warning in Hebrews 5:11. Here the writer says in effect: 'I was getting ready to talk to you about Melchizedek but I can't go on, seeing that I have many difficult things to say and you are dull of hearing.'

Isaiah said, 'Seek ye the Lord while he may be found, call ye upon him while he is near' (Is. 55:6).

What we are talking about is the ability to recognise and respond to the Spirit's impulse. I consider this to be the highest level of spirituality that exists.

Are we able to see the work of the Spirit? Would we recognise revival if we saw it or heard about it? If God poured out his Spirit in some unexpected place, would we still recognise him? Do we know when God is speaking to us? Can we sense the way he is leading us? The spiritual ability to recognise the Spirit's impulse comes from listening to and hearing God.

I want to approach this subject from the general and then move on to the particular. By general, I mean knowing how to listen to God anywhere – at home, at work on a train, seven days a week, twenty-four hours a day.

I would like to put to you a premise that is hard to accept, yet is thrilling and true: God is trying to get us to listen to him. It was A. W. Tozer who said, 'We can have as much of God as we want.' Some people may deny this. They say that if it were true, they would know it. But it is affirmed seven times in Revelation chapters 2 and 3. Each time Jesus gave a particular word to the church, he added, 'Hear what the Spirit saith unto the churches.' God is constantly trying to get the churches' attention.

It's very interesting that after Jesus addressed all seven churches with the words, 'Hear what the Spirit saith,' he then narrowed the invitation down to one person and said, 'If any man hear my voice, and open the door, I will come in to him, and will sup with him, and he with me' (Rev. 3:20).

Someone may protest, 'My problem is getting God to listen to me. I identify with the psalmist when he said, "Hear me when I call, O God of my righteousness: thou hast enlarged me when I was in distress; have mercy upon me and hear my prayer" (Ps. 4:1). That's where I am. I'm always asking God to hear me.'

Maybe you feel like the people who said, 'O God, we have fasted and you didn't even notice!' (see Is. 58:3). It is possible to spend hours every day talking to God like this. But the problem is that it is *we* who are doing all the talking, all the thinking, all the groaning and we shut God out. We think we are open to him when in fact we are only talking to him. And all the time he may be wanting to communicate with us at the level that we need, not at the level at which we are addressing him. We want to talk about one thing and God is saying, 'That's not your problem; your problem is over here.' We are looking in one direction and he's trying to get us to look in another.

Now when anyone develops a hearing problem, it usually doesn't happen overnight. It is a gradual and almost unnoticed event. And the same thing is true at the spiritual level: we hardly know it is happening. In the end we have to be jolted and made to realise what has been going on. It is like not realising we have been asleep until we wake up.

There are two reasons why God has difficulty in getting us to listen to him. The first is our inability to absorb or take in his counsel. Jesus said it like this: 'I have yet many things to say unto you, but ye cannot bear them now' (John 16:12). His disciples wouldn't have admitted to that. They would have said, 'Try me. See if I can't take it. Speak plainly.' But Jesus said, 'You couldn't take it.' We all overestimate our capacity to grasp and take in things, not realising that if God were to tell us all there is to know, our minds would snap. God has to deal with us where we are.

People come into the vestry and say, 'Do you think you know what my problem is?'

Seven or eight years ago I made the mistake of saying to one peson, 'Yes, I think I do.'

This person said, 'Well, what is it?'

It was an awful moment. I said, 'I think we ought to talk a little more over several weeks.'

He said, 'Come on. Tell me. I can take it.'

So I told him.

He said, 'You are direct, aren't you?' And he never came back.

I should have known better. From many years of pastoral experience I have learned that people don't want their problems solved. They want them understood. We are all like that and God knows it.

The second reason why God has difficulty in getting us to listen to him is that there is uncleansed sin within us as a result of not walking in the light. We say, 'Lord, speak to me.'

God answers, 'I did speak but you wouldn't take it.'

We say, 'I didn't want that. Lord, speak to me.'

'I am speaking.'

'No, Lord, speak to me.'

A lady once came to Arthur Blessitt and asked him, 'Why doesn't God speak to me like he seems to speak to you?'

And Arthur said to her, 'Did you ever feel the impulse to speak to a stranger about the Lord but then were ashamed and didn't do it?'

When the lady replied, 'Yes, I have,' Arthur said, 'Well that's your problem. When you start to obey the impulse of the Spirit God's voice gets clearer and clearer.'

God is trying to reach us and we hear him to the degree that we are walking in the light. Is it possible that God is trying to speak to you along a certain line but you are saying, 'I know God wouldn't say that to me'?

Here's a verse that none of us likes: 'Then shall they also answer him, saying, Lord when saw we thee an hungred, or athirst, or a stranger, or naked, or sick, or in prison, and did not minister unto thee? Then shall he answer them, saying, Verily I say unto you, Inasmuch as ye did it not to one of the least of these, ye did it not to me' (Matt. 25:44–45). When we get to the judgment the Lord could look at us in much the same way and remind us of certain areas of our life and we will be speechless. It's very important that we should be transparently honest with ourselves.

The final tragic result of disobedience, of course, is that God stops speaking to us. One of the saddest verses in the Bible is 1 Samuel 28:15, where Saul says, 'God is departed from me, and answereth me no more.'

There are two kinds of listening: active listening and passive listening.

By passive listening I mean when we suddenly,

unexpectedly hear the voice of God without planning it or seeking it. If there is a combination of a good knowledge of God's word, plus obedience, then the ecstatic breakthrough may come and come quite unexpectedly. Hearing God in this way happens less frequently than hearing God as a result of active listening, but most of us want only passive listening. We want God to seek us out. That way we don't work hard at hearing God, but when he taps us on the shoulder we say, 'Praise the Lord! He's still speaking to me.'

But passive hearing is not the primary way God speaks to us. God calls us to active listening: 'Hear what the Spirit says . . .' The writer to the Hebrews said, 'Strong meat belongeth to them that are of full age, even those who by reason of use have their senses exercised to discern both good and evil' (Heb. 5:14). Exercised senses come through active listening.

The first quality required for active listening is an open mind. That means, a mind closed to nothing that coheres with holiness. Paul says about this, 'Finally, brethren, whatsoever things are true, whatsoever things are honest, whatsoever things are just, whatsoever things are pure, whatsoever things are lovely, whatsoever things are of good report; if there be any virtue, and if there be any praise, think on these things' (Phil. 4:8).

The second prerequisite for active listening is a willingness to let go of our pride, a willingness to be vulnerable. Jesus said to the church of the Laodiceans, 'Thou sayest, I am rich, and increased with goods, and have need of nothing . . .' and the truth is, says Jesus, '. . . thou art wretched, and miserable, and poor, and blind, and naked' (Rev. 3:17). I sometimes think that revival will break out when Christians are willing to lose face. Jesus said, 'He that loseth his life for my sake shall find it' (Matt. 10:39).

The third characteristic is that we are always listening out for God's voice, even when this involves a telling off.

Jesus said, 'As many as I love, I rebuke and chasten: be zealous therefore, and repent' (Rev. 3:19). God may speak to us through a friend, or a stranger; through unanswered prayer, or through the withholding of vindication. It may be through illness. It may be through a hymn: 'Sometimes a light surprises the Christian while he sings . . .' It may be through disappointment. It can be simply because you see the need. If we are really walking in the light we will look anywhere for God's way of speaking.

Unfortunately, many of us say, 'If I have to believe that anybody could be God's instrument in my life, then forget it. There are some people I draw the line at.' Yet Paul said, 'I am a debtor . . . both to the wise, and to the unwise' (Rom. 1:14).

Sometimes we deceive ourselves without realising it. We think we are openly and actively listening to God, when we are actually blinkered. As I have said, so often we expect God to speak to us in one way, when all the time he is approaching us differently. Someone has put it like this: God gives hints rather than directions. He lets you come to the conclusion for yourself.

John the Baptist wanted more than a hint; he wanted clear direction. In prison he had a moment of discouragement, even though once he had said, 'Behold the Lamb of God, which taketh away the sin of the world' (John 1:29). He had second thoughts and sent back word to Jesus, 'Art thou he that should come? or look we for another?' (Luke 7:19). Imagine John the Baptist talking like that! You would have thought that Jesus would have replied: 'Tell John, yes, I'm the one.' But he didn't answer like that. He just said, 'Tell John what things ye have seen and heard; how that the blind see, the lame walk, the lepers are cleansed, the deaf hear, the dead are raised, to the poor the gospel is preached' (Luke 7:22). This was a clear hint. And that's the way God deals with all of us.

The fourth prerequisite to hearing God is that we deal

with any impediment that militates against the Spirit, for example, any personal bias which we superimpose upon God, calling it his will when it's actually our own prejudice, and any grudge or unforgiving attitude.

I remember receiving a letter from a lady I had never met but who had heard me preach on Joseph and his brothers. I preached on the concept of total forgiveness, by which I mean totally forgiving the other person, no matter who it is or what has been done. I said that to the degree you don't forgive, no matter how wronged you are, you are the one in chains.

She wrote me a long letter saying, 'Let me tell you what's happened to me . . .' A relative had done something really wicked twenty-five years ago, and this lady said, 'I can't forgive but your sermon made me wonder if I should.'

I wrote back and said, 'You must.'

Some weeks later she wrote again and said, 'I never thought I could do it, but I did and the joy is wonderful.'

We may justify our hurt, and say that God is angry too. We may think he is, because that's the way we want him to feel, but he's not going to bend the rules for us, even if we are in the right. Total forgiveness is our only way out. If we walk in the light we are going to have to forgive. If we don't forgive there will be uncleansed sin.

Another impediment that militates against hearing God speaking is when we superimpose our traditions upon the word of God. This is what the Pharisees did when they made the word of God of none effect through their traditions (Matt. 16:6). I will be returning to this subject in Chapter 21.

Again, we must beware of any fleshly appetite that dulls our spiritual outlook: it may be a television programme, our choice of reading or of friends. Some things may not be bad in themselves, but we know that they dull our desire for God. Though others may think we are silly, we know that if we want to hear God's voice consistently and clearly, we must be willing to give some things up.

Finally, as we have already seen, we must obey that impulse of the Spirit which we know leads to holiness and brings honour and glory to God. If we don't obey, we become hard of hearing, and gradually don't hear God saying, 'This is the way, walk ye in it.'

To sum up the difference between active and passive listening: active listening is reading the Bible without feeling any inspiration. There are times when we don't feel like reading the Bible. We think, 'Oh, Lord, I don't want to read your word today.' But we go on and read God's word in spite of our feelings, because Paul said, 'Be instant in season, out of season' (2 Tim. 4:2).

When we learn to develop a lifestyle of active listening we will hear God's voice much more frequently than before, because now we are beginning to recognise when he speaks.

I know from personal experience that it can sometimes take an embarrassing number of years before we recognise that God has been speaking to us. Eventually we say, 'That really was God speaking to me then. I didn't know it, but I see now it was.'

Whenever we have a violent reaction to something, we must be alert to the possibility that God might be wanting to teach us something. We say, 'God wouldn't say that to me!' And it might take us ten years before we realise our mistake.

My first reaction to Evangelism Explosion in 1964 was that it was fleshly, and I spoke against Dr James Kennedy. I'm so ashamed now – but he loved me right through it all.

Let me give you some practical advice: write down in detail a list of questions you would like God to answer. They may be theological or practical. I've done this. I have a prayer list with the theological questions I'm asking. 'Lord, tell me the truth about what I should believe in detail about grace or the law. Do I really have to affirm predestination or the doctrine of election? Show me the truth about baptism or what I need to know about hell and heaven or the doctrine of the Church.' Write them out and pray over them every single day for a year.

Then write out the practical questions. 'Lord, do you want me to get this job? Do you want me to go there? Do you want me to apply for this? Do you want me to see this person?' Write them out and pray over them every day for one year. Then twelve months from now, if you spend the time actively listening to God, see how many of your questions have been answered.

To return, now, to worship and listening to God at church. If we have been listening this way all day, seven days a week, when we come to church we continue in the same way.

As far as is possible, we must come to church in an open state of mind. Sometimes we come with a very burdened and preoccupied heart and we forget how difficult it is for God to speak to us when we are like that. It's best if we can put our own concerns in suspension so that God can speak to us in the way he wants to. It may then turn out that he will deal with the problem we had.

We must come expecting God to speak to us. We must trust the Holy Spirit to have directed the preacher in his choice of hymns or choruses, the reading, the preaching, the sermon material. And we must receive God's word with openness and humility. We must, of course, listen critically to what the preacher is saying. No minister should produce a congregation of rubber stamps – that would cut right across the doctrine of the priesthood of all believers. Each person in the congregation must think for himself or herself and assess whether what the preacher is saying is true or not. But if we listen with a defensive, aggressive or spiteful attitude, then we will quench the Spirit before he can even speak.

Then, we must listen prayerfully – we must know the

art of listening and praying at the same time. We must always be aware that powers from below would work against the preaching. So we must pray continually for the preacher as he preaches, and for ourselves to have the grace to receive what the Spirit is saying. The minister and his congregation are all in it together. It is not just a matter of saying, 'I wonder if he's going to preach well today?' Someone who is only a sermon taster will not worship God.

But if we come longing to hear God speaking to us, actively and prayerfully listening for him, in humility and dependence on his Spirit, then true worship will take place.

CHAPTER 7

EXPECTANCY

'And when they had prayed, the place was shaken where they were assembled together . . .' (Acts 4:31)

I concluded Chapter 6 by talking about how important it is to come to church longing to hear God speaking. This is so crucial that I want to return to it. A vital ingredient of worship is expectancy: believing that something good is going to happen. Nothing is sadder than going to church when you aren't expecting anything to happen, and even know that nothing is going to happen. When you feel that way – what a surprise – nothing does happen! Yet so many people throughout the world go to church feeling like that. It is not surprising that churches are closing down. You would be shocked if you knew how many evangelical churches in Britain have not had a conversion in five years – and are not even expecting to see any conversions.

Of course, we have just as great a need for expectancy in our private devotional life. When you come to read your Bible and pray, do you expect something to happen? The peak moment of my day is when I can be alone with God. I get out my Bible and expect God to speak to me. Every time I open my Bible, I think, 'Lord, what are you going to say to me today?'

And when I feel this way, and look for God to speak,

then he often does. This is how it should be with everyone. No one should come to pray thinking, 'Oh, I suppose I've got to pray.' How dare we claim to love God if coming to him is a duty!

In Acts 4 we read that a number of people – we don't know exactly how many – were gathered together to pray. What is remarkable is what happened as soon as they had finished praying. Verse 31 says, 'And when they had prayed, the place was shaken . . .' What an extraordinary comment. Nothing like that had ever happened before. It was not that the people were shaken – though I have no doubt they were – but 'the place was shaken where they were assembled together; and they were all filled with the Holy Ghost, and they spake the word of God with boldness.'

In this passage we have a description of an expectant people – and this for four reasons.

First, they were converted people. Why mention this? It's because I wish to say that if we ever lose that sense of expectancy, we must recall that we are converted – which means that at least once God did something in our lives. These people who were filled with the Holy Spirit had already had that experience once. Never think that something can only happen once. Even the baptism of the Holy Spirit can happen again and again. When you are discouraged, and find yourself saying, 'I haven't been seeing anything happen to me,' remember that you are converted. That ought to keep up your sense of expectancy for if God saved you and me, he can save anybody.

The second reason why these people were expectant is that they had seen God work recently. In Acts 3 we have the account of the miracle of the healing of the lame man. In a sense this miracle was the worst thing that could have happened to the Church. You would think that a miracle would make everybody happy. But not at all. When something like that happens, than all the so-called religious people vent their hatred on the people of God. And I suspect that if similar miracles were to happen today they would get the Church into just as much trouble.

Everybody had seen God work, not only at the level of healing, but also in the miracle of conversion, which, of course, is the greatest miracle of all. And numbers in the church were growing – chapter 4:4 speaks of 'about five thousand' people. It is important for us to see God at work continuously, and it is a wonderful experience when people are converted in our church services. When we have seen God working, we expect him to continue working.

One of my great joys is fishing. All year I fish for men, but for my summer holiday we go to the Florida Keys and I fish for fish. It is very discouraging to hear people saying, 'There's no use going out – no one's catching anything. We were out all day yesterday and got nothing.' (Discouraging, that is, unless you're as determined as I am. Nothing will stop me, and I go out anyway!)

But if everyone says, 'They're all over the place! Everywhere we were yesterday, there were bonefish tailing on this flat – on that flat . . . !' Then you go out expecting something to happen. When I hear that, and I know that the wind is right and the tide is right and the water temperature is right, I get so excited that I can hardly sleep the night before!

It is the same in our churches. When we have seen something happen, as these people in Acts had, we look to God for it to happen again.

But, thirdly, the people had also just seen the devil stirred up. We read in verse 18 that the religious officials had called Peter and John in and 'commanded them not to speak at all nor teach in the name of Jesus'. And the devil was behind that. For whenever the church regroups to evangelise, you can mark it down that the devil will be angry. Many things the Church gets involved with pose no threat to the devil, and he stays at bay. But once you propose to invade his territory, you have a fight on your hands. When the devil is stirred up it is a good sign, because it shows he is afraid that something is going to happen.

The final reason why these people were expectant is that they knew what God was able to do. This is why they prayed as they did. Verses 23 and 24 say, 'And being let go, they [Peter and John] went to their own company, and reported all that the chief priests and elders had said unto them. And when they heard that, they lifted up their voice to God with one accord.' They had their backs against the wall, but they had a momentum derived from seeing God work beyond the natural level.

Many churches can never think other than at the natural level. What about our resources? Who do we know? Who can pull this string for us? But here was a group who only had God to back them up. Five thousand may sound a large number of people – but they were a tiny minority in the country at the time – and they were hated and despised by the authorities. They didn't have powerful friends in the Sanhedrin who would stand up for them. They had no one in Caesar's government. But they had God. So they were expectant.

I suspect that most of us haven't a clue about what it really means to be expectant, and to rely on God alone. So let's look more closely at this prayer in Acts 4 – a prayer that resulted in a building being shaken!

First, in this prayer we see the unity of the people. Verse 24 says that they 'lifted up their voice to God with one accord'. Unity is of vital importance in worship. The people here had achieved their unity by coming together against a common enemy. But this unity also required magnanimity. You can be sure that they had differences among themselves – everybody does. (And the less you have of the Spirit, the more important will those differences seem.) But they knew that the devil was against them so they put their differences aside. Would to God that the Church at the present time would do the same.

The issue at stake here was that the witnessing should not stop. The authorities had told Peter and John that they would not be put in prison for what they believed, but that they were to keep it to themselves: 'They . . . commanded them not to speak at all nor teach in the name of Jesus' (v.18). If these early Christians had been like some of us today, someone would have stood up and said, 'Look here, Peter and John, we think you're carrying this a bit too far. We've done our piece. We've done a bit of witnessing and shown that we could do it. But now we've upset the Sanhedrin, and they are learned and respected men. So let's cool it for a while.'

But not one person said anything like that. Instead, they lifted up their voices to God with one accord. If the Church had become divided at that point, the book of Acts would have ended right there. There is no substitute for witnessing.

The second aspect of the expectancy of these people is that they uttered their longings. They put their words on the line. It is easy to keep one's thoughts to oneself. Other people can't hold us accountable for what we've not said. But these early Christians shared what was in their minds.

The NIV says, 'They raised their voices.' I don't think I've ever heard that in our church prayer meetings. I never hear more than one person pray at one time. Are we afraid to speak out all at once?

In Korea the Christians are seeing God at work, and a film has been made about the revival there. In this film we see the minister of a church lead in prayer, and everyone starts praying. I don't suppose the people even knew what the minister was saying. It's a noisy meeting.

Could it be that revival has come to the Third World and passed us by because we are too sophisticated? In those churches in Korea they are not ashamed to cry aloud to God. Most of our praying is shameful: 'Heavenly Father, we come to you . . . we pray for your blessing upon us and . . . to have your way . . . in our hearts and lives . . . and . . . and . . .'

There is no indication in our language that we expect to see God do anything. I'm not saying that this would bring revival. I'm only saying that this is what they knew in Acts, when the Spirit was present. Perhaps our problem is that we're just too comfortable.

The third thing we can see about this prayer is its upward direction: 'They lifted up their voice to God.' It didn't cross their minds to look to one another. Yes – they talked to one another, but how long do you think the 'committee meeting' lasted? Verse 23 says, 'And being let go, they went to their own company, and reported all that the chief priests and elders had said unto them.' I suppose that took about five minutes, and then they were on their faces.

We are in the day of committees and conferences. 'The merry-go-rounds of conferences,' as it has been put. We don't see God work, but we're great at talking to one another. When these people heard what Peter and John had to say, they didn't have to debate it. They just said, 'Let's pray.'

I never will forget the night three or four years ago when Dr O. S. Hawkins said he would take my wife and me out for a meal after the deacons' meeting at his church. He said, 'We'll just be a little while.'

I thought he'd be at least a couple of hours, but about twenty-five minutes later he appeared and said, 'Are you ready to go?'

When I expressed my surprise that he was so early, he asked me to take a look in at the meeting – and there were twenty-five deacons on their knees, praying. He said, 'That's the way our deacons' meetings go.'

I fear that the importance of prayer hasn't begun to grip many of our churches like this.

The fourth thing about this prayer is the understanding that undergirded their expectancy. There are three things here. First, what these people understood about

God. Verse 24 says, 'And when they heard that, they lifted up their voice to God with one accord, and said, "Lord, thou art God, which hast made heaven, and earth, and the sea, and all that in them is."' The people knew that God made the world and everything in it: he is the all-powerful Creator.

Secondly, these people believed that God wrote the Bible. Verse 25 says, 'Who by the mouth of thy servant David hast said, Why did the heathen rage . . . ?' As Calvin said, one of the best ways to pray is just to quote God's word back to him.

The third thing is their belief in God's sovereignty. Verses 27 and 28 say, 'For of a truth against thy holy child Jesus, whom thou hast anointed, both Herod and Pontius Pilate, with the Gentiles, and the people of Israel, were gathered together. For to do whatsoever thy hand and thy counsel determined before to be done.' This is a crucial point. They saw God in everything. When the crucifixion took place, the disciples hadn't been able to see God's hand in it at all. All they could say was, 'Isn't it horrible that this has happened to Jesus!' But now they could look back and say, 'God did it.' Satan filled the heart of Judas Iscariot. Wicked men led Pontius Pilate to do what he did. But God was behind it all.

1 Corinthians 2:7–8 says, 'But we speak the wisdom of God in a mystery, even the hidden wisdom, which God ordained before the world unto our glory: which none of the princes of this world knew: for had they known it, they would not have crucified the Lord of glory.'

But Satan always overreaches himself. And the angrier Satan is, the more you ought to look for God's sovereign overruling. These people had seen what God had done through the crucifixion of Jesus, and they could see now that Satan was at work again. But they were not panicking, because they knew that Satan never catches God off guard. The expectancy of these early Christians was clothed with a robust view of God's sovereign purposes.

Finally, their expectancy had an urgency. The key word is 'now'. Look at verse 29: 'And now, Lord, behold their threatenings.' Sometimes God brings us to the place where we have to see him act *now*. Urgency always means, 'Lord, do it now!' They weren't asking for the conditions to be removed so that they wouldn't have to be witnesses any more. They simply wanted boldness to witness, and they prayed for God to do again what he had done before. They had already seen signs and wonders, and that had got them into a heap of trouble, but they said, 'Lord, do it again!' They wanted God to give a fresh display of his power.

And God's response to the prayer of the people was that the place was shaken. Never before had they seen anything like it. And it has not occurred since. Sometimes God just likes to do something once. Joshua saw the sun stand still for twenty-four hours. It never happened again. On the day of Pentecost 'cloven tongues like as of fire' came on the heads of the people. It happened once. God may do something with us which will never be repeated. And if our expectancy is at the level of these people in Acts 4, who knows what it might be?

All this was the consequence of their expectancy and trust in God. May God grant that such expectancy may be in all our church services and prayer meetings. Then perhaps we too will see the unprecedented, or, at the very least, what we long for: a demonstration of God's power which defies natural explanation.

CHAPTER 8

WORSHIPPING IN THE DARK

'Although the fig tree shall not blossom, neither shall fruit be in the vines . . . yet I will rejoice in the Lord, I will joy in the God of my salvation.' (Habakkuk 3:17–18)

As we have just seen in Chapter 7, expectancy is a vital ingredient in worship. Those who come to church expecting something to happen are more likely to see God work than those who come expecting nothing. But what about when we do come with expectancy, and nothing happens? What about when we feel God has let us down? We say, 'God, I came today and I wanted you to speak, but you didn't speak to me!' What can we say about times like these?

The same questions apply to our own quiet times with God. Maybe we've prayed every day during the week and yet have not experienced God's blessing or seen him answer prayer. What then?

My answer is that faithfulness is, if anything, even more important than expectancy in worship: 'It is required in stewards [that is, those who have been given a trust] that a man [or woman] be found faithful' (1 Cor. 4:2). 'A faithful man who can find?' asks the writer of Proverbs (Prov. 20:6). Anybody can be faithful when prayer is being answered, when the wind is at one's back and everything is going well. But what is one to do when God suddenly hides his face?

We have all experienced this. If you are a new Christian and haven't yet – you will! 'Verily thou art a God that hidest thyself, O God of Israel, the Saviour,' said Isaiah (Is. 45:15).

The thing about the hiding of the face of God is that it never comes with advance warning. If only I could say to my church members, 'I need to make an announcement. This week it is going to be on Wednesday. At about a quarter past eleven you will notice the withdrawal of the light of God's countenance, and you will feel desperate. You are going to be on the brink of despair. You are going to call upon the name of God and receive no reply. Things are going to go wrong. You will feel utterly deserted. It will happen, as I said, on Wednesday morning.'

If I could do that, everyone would brace themselves for it. It would be like getting a hurricane or a storm warning. But the thing about the hiding of God's face is that we don't expect it.

And it can happen when we are not aware that we have done anything wrong. God does, of course, hide his face when we are disobeying him – but when that happens, we understand it. What is particularly painful is when we are doing our best to walk in the light, and God hides his face.

The night before Martin Luther was due to stand before the authorities of Rome, who had charged him with heresy, when everybody had turned their backs on him, he walked the floor of his room and cried out, 'O my God, art thou dead?' You would have thought that God would have been especially real to Martin Luther at that time. You would have thought that since God had chosen Luther to be the man who would turn the world upside down, on that particular night he would have given Luther an extra measure of his Spirit. But Luther felt utterly deserted.

The following day he said the famous words, 'Here I stand.' It sounds triumphant, but Luther was scared to death.

They asked him, 'Dr Luther, are these your tracts?'

He said, 'Yes, they are.'

'Will you recant what you have said?'

'Yes, I will if you can show that they are contrary to the word of God, but if you can't, here I stand. I can do no other. God help me. Amen.'

He was scared to death. He had no sense of God's presence but he was faithful.

I never will forget what I went through way back in 1956. I came back from Trevecca Nazarene College in Nashville, to my home in Ashland, Kentucky, with a discovery of the sovereign grace of God. I thought my family would clap their hands and say, 'This is marvellous.' But no. My family deserted me.

A few years ago, as minister of Westminster Chapel, I thought that if we went on with God and were more involved in evangelism, those who had supported me in the past would be behind me, but many weren't.

We don't understand why it is, but sometimes when we obey God, he seems to desert us. Martin Luther said that you must know God as an enemy before you can know him as a friend. Until you have experienced the hiding of his face and come out on the other side, you won't really come to know God as a friend.

This was Habakkuk's experience. Habakkuk 2:4 is a famous verse which is quoted three times in the New Testament: 'The just shall live by his faith.' In the Hebrew this reads: 'The just shall live by his faithfulness.'

There is an intentional ambiguity here. The faithfulness can be God's faithfulness to us, or our faithfulness to God: the verse can be read either way, and it means both. In the Dead Sea Scrolls, discovered in 1947, there is a commentary on Habakkuk 2:4, and it reads, 'The just shall live by God's faithfulness.' This refers to living by the fact that God is faithful to his promises. It is the way Hebrews 10:38 interprets this verse.

But it can equally describe the faithfulness of the individual himself, who doesn't give up hope. The person who trusts God, and lives by his promise to bless, is declared righteous in the sight of God. That became one of the main verses Paul used for the doctrine of justification by faith. It applies to the future – to the fact that God will accept us in heaven – but it also applies to the present. God is saying that we are declared righteous now. There is an existential element here. The word 'existential' means existence – the here and now. What needs to be seen from this verse in Habakkuk is that as we live by God's faithfulness we are in each moment being declared righteous.

If we could only see this today, it would set us afire. If, in the moment when we don't see answered prayer, we could just look up to heaven and say, 'God, I love you anyway,' God would declare us righteous just because our faith pleases him. That kind of faith has a cleansing result. We feel clean. We don't understand why God lets things happen, but we trust him anyway.

I want to illustrate this in the context of the book of Habakkuk. Just before writing these words, 'The just shall live by his faithfulness,' Habakkuk says, 'For the vision is yet for an appointed time . . . though it tarry, wait for it' (v.3). The key phrase is, 'though it tarry, wait for it'. This principle even applies partly to the Second Coming of Jesus. Jesus said, 'If that evil servant shall say in his heart, My lord delayeth his coming; and shall begin to smite his fellowservants, and to eat and drink with the drunken; the lord of that servant shall come in a day when he looketh not for him, and in an hour that he is not aware of, and shall cut him asunder, and appoint him his portion with the hypocrites: there shall be weeping and gnashing of teeth' (Matt. 24:48–51).

When Jesus comes again, or when God comes to fulfil any promise he has made to us, will he find us patiently waiting for him?

After Jesus was raised from the dead, he addressed 500

at once (1 Cor. 15:6). And on the Day of Pentecost there were 120 praying in the Upper Room. I believe more than 120 people could have been there. I believe that on the first day when Jesus went to heaven they all went to Jerusalem to wait for the promised Spirit. There were probably 500 people, all very excited. Then after a couple of days they began to drift away, so that when the Day of Pentecost arrived there were only 120. How do you suppose the others felt when they found out what had happened and realised that they had missed out?

Many people make a commitment in a moment of inspiration and get a good feeling, but months later that dwindles away. There is an appalling lack of commitment in so many. People start out saying, 'Yes, Lord,' then six months later, where are they? It's true with church attendance, with witness on the streets, with tithing, with prayer.

The wider context of Habakkuk shows that there were those who were complaining that God wasn't acting quickly enough. Habakkuk didn't understand either. Elijah was 'a man subject to like passions as we are' (James 5:17). So was Habakkuk. He had questions and doubts. But though he began with complaint, he ended with rejoicing. Chapter 1:2 says, 'O Lord, how long shall I cry, and thou wilt not hear!' But at the end of the book Habakkuk says, 'The Lord God is my strength, and he will make my feet like hinds' feet, and he will make me to walk upon mine high places' (3:19). He began by complaining and he ended by rejoicing.

What happened between the beginning of the book of Habakkuk and the end? Someone might say, 'Obviously things must have changed.' But did they? Look at chapter 3:17–18: 'Although the fig tree shall not blossom, neither shall fruit be in the vines; the labour of the olive shall fail, and the fields shall yield no meat; the flock shall be cut off from the fold, and there shall be no herd in the stalls: yet I will rejoice in the Lord, I will joy in the God of my salvation.' The basis for the complaint was still there. The very things Habakkuk had complained about, he could still complain about. The fig tree wasn't blossoming. There was no fruit, no herd in the stalls – and yet he was rejoicing. He wasn't complaining now. What changed his mind?

We need to see, first of all, the nature of Habakkuk's complaint. First, he complained about God's slowness: 'O Lord, how long shall I cry?' (1:2). It makes me think of that verse in Revelation 6:10 which says, 'And they cried with aloud voice, saying, How long, O Lord, holy and true, dost thou not judge and avenge our blood on them that dwell on the earth?' In Psalm 13 we read, 'How long wilt thou forget me, O Lord? for ever? how long wilt thou hide thy face from me?'

The question, 'How long?' is a familiar question among us all. For most of us God never acts quickly enough. Have you ever asked the question: why is God slow? One reason is that he sees the end from the beginning. Knowing how it's going to end up, he is in no hurry. Another reason is that time is on his side. Also, as the Bible says, 'One day is with the Lord as a thousand years, and a thousand years as one day' (2 Pet. 3:8). God is in no hurry. He is patient.

And very often we are glad that God is patient. Aren't there times when we thank him for being slow to anger and rich in mercy? How would we like it if God stepped in the moment we sinned? The time comes later when we blush and say, 'God, I'm sorry. I was wrong.'

And God says, 'I knew you were wrong, but I knew you would eventually see it.'

Then we say, 'Thank you, Lord, for being so patient with me.'

Habakkuk also complained that God did nothing while injustice thrived. The NIV translates 1:3 as: 'Why do you make me look at injustice? Why do you tolerate wrong?' Don't think that it's only the atheist who questions God about suffering.

The atheist says, 'I'll tell you why I don't believe in God . . .' And he is proud of himself for coming up with such a devastating question: why does God allow suffering? But Habakkuk, a godly man, said, 'Lord, why do you tolerate wrong?' and for a long time God didn't answer. He was silent.

But then, at last, God stepped in. He told Habakkuk that he would send an evil nation, the Chaldeans, to destroy his people. There does come a time when God acts. One after another the prophets all hoped to see the coming of the Messiah, and eventually, after hundreds of years the Messiah came. As Paul put it: 'When the fulness of the time was come, God sent forth his Son, made of a woman, made under the law' (Gal. 4:4).

In chapter 2 Habakkuk is getting hold of himself. He says, 'I'm going to wait and see what God will say.' Three things consoled him. The first was that he could see that God saw what he saw: 'The Lord answered me, and said, Write the vision-and make it plain upon tables, that he may run that readeth it' (v.2). What a relief just to know that God sees!

Hagar, when she was ill-treated by Sarah, looked to heaven and said, 'Thou God seest me' (Gen. 16:13) – it is one of the most moving scenes in the Bible.

And that is what God said to Moses: 'I have surely seen the affliction of my people' (Ex. 3:7). Nothing is more consoling than to know that God sees. I think that most people come into the vestry to talk to me because they want me to listen and say, 'I understand.' When we know that God sees, we can make it.

The second thing that consoled Habakkuk was the knowledge that though full intervention might not come as soon as he wanted – 'Though it tarry, wait for it' (Hab. 2:3) – it would nevertheless definitely come. There was a plan; there was a time schedule. God said to Habakkuk: There is an appointed time. Maybe it's a little longer than you want it to be, but wait for it, it will come. That knowledge gave Habakkuk a good feeling.

The third thing that consoled Habakkuk was the understanding that God imputes righteousness to the man or woman who lives by God's faithfulness. We have already observed that this was the foundation for the Pauline doctrine of justification by faith alone. When we say, 'God, I don't understand it. I don't know why you have let me wait this long. I don't know why you haven't stepped in sooner. But I am trusting you,' we are cleansed in that moment and are given rest of soul. We sense that behind the clouds the sun is shining and God does see us. He says, 'I like it when you trust me that way.'

Sometimes in prayer and Bible reading we feel no inspiration, and to continue is almost like drudgery. When I first went to Oxford in 1973, my supervisor, Dr Barrie White, said, 'It's the drudgery of it that you are going to have to endure.' And did I have an inferiority complex during those first weeks and months at Oxford! I come from the hills of Kentucky, and I don't think too many people make it to England or Oxford from there. I could see why after I was there. I wondered, 'What am I doing here?' I thought, 'O God, will I ever get through?' I was at sea, and it was drudgery. I would go every day to the Bodleian Library. I spent twenty-five hours a day in the Bodleian for about two hundred years, it seemed, reading William Perkins and William Ames every day. 'Is it worth it?' I asked.

But the breakthrough came. Without the drudgery there would have been no light at the end of the tunnel, no rainbow to trace through the rain. It's when you are faithful daily in everything because it is right that God makes a note of it, and payday comes some day.

At the end of the book of Habakkuk the prophet is a changed man. Look at his confidence: 'Although the fig tree shall not blossom, neither shall fruit be in the vines; the labour of the olive shall fail, and the fields shall yield no meat; the flock shall be cut off from the fold, and there shall be no herd in the stalls; yet I will rejoice in the Lord' – he says it twice – 'I will joy in the God of my salvation. The Lord God is my strength, and he will make my feet like hinds' feet, and he will make me to walk upon mine high places' (3:17–19). That is how confident Habakkuk became.

Are you looking for the vine to blossom before you can rejoice? Are you looking for the fig tree to give figs before you can praise the Lord? Are you waiting for the rise in pay? Or for that answered prayer? Are you waiting for everything to fit in before you start praising the Lord? If that is so, then turn in your badge now and give up. As Proverbs 24:10 says, 'If thou faint in the day of adversity, thy strength is small.' Here was Habakkuk who still had all these complaints but yet said, 'I will rejoice.'

Nothing changed outwardly. The basis for Habakkuk's complaints was still there, the injustices were still there. Nothing had happened to them, but a lot happened to him. Habakkuk was given grace to trace the rainbow through the rain.

Habakkuk saw something that we all need to see: that grace will always be there to keep us one step ahead of the enemy. At the beginning when he talked about the Babylonians, he said, 'Their horses also are swifter than the leopards' (1:8), but now he says, 'God will make my feet like hinds' feet' (3:19). Whereas a horse can run fast, a deer can climb to places a horse cannot reach. Grace will always be given to us so that we can be one step ahead of the enemy. As Moses said, 'As thy days, so shall thy strength be' (Deut. 33:25).

The soul that on Jesus has leaned for repose
I will not, I will not desert to its foes;
That soul, though all hell should endeavour to shake,
I'll never, no never, no never, forsake!

Things may not get better around us – but a lot can happen to us – and that changes everything.

CHAPTER 9

WORSHIP AT THE LORD'S TABLE

'And they continued stedfastly in the apostles' doctrine and fellowship and in breaking of bread . . .' (Acts 2:42)

No other act of worship in the Church carries a warning like the one which Paul gives in 1 Corinthians 11:29 concerning the Lord's Supper. Paul says, 'For he that eateth and drinketh unworthily, eateth and drinketh damnation [Greek: judgment] to himself, not discerning the Lord's body.' No such warning is attached to praying or singing, to fellowship or doctrine, important though these are. This shows that the Lord's Supper has an exalted place in God's plan for man.

Yet what do we really know about worship at the Lord's Table? If we don't know a lot, perhaps it will be of some comfort to us to hear that the Christians at Corinth do not seem to have known much. And we can learn from their errors.

In 1 Corinthians 11:17–32 Paul says: 'Now in this that I declare unto you I praise you not, that ye come together not for the better, but for the worse.' Or, as the NIV puts it: 'I have no praise for you, for your meetings do more harm than good.'

In verses 17–32 of chapter 11, Paul mentions three things which were wrong with the church at Corinth, and the first is that there were divisions among them. He says,

'For there must be also heresies among you, that they which are approved may be made manifest among you' (v.19). I know of no translation of this verse which adequately brings out the fact that Paul is rebuking the Corinthians for maintaining that they needed these divisions and cliques. With biting sarcasm, Paul is saying, '*You* need to have *divisions* to show which of you has God's approval!'

Similarly, back in chapter 4:8, Paul said, 'Now ye are full, now ye are rich, ye have reigned as kings without us.' Here again, Paul is telling the Corinthians off, as we can see from the solemn warning he gives in chapter 4:4–5: 'For I know nothing by myself; yet am I not hereby justified: but he that judgeth me is the Lord. Therefore judge nothing before the time, until the Lord come, who both will bring to light the hidden things of darkness, and will make manifest the counsels of the hearts: and then shall every man have praise of God.' Chapter 11 reveals that the people could not wait for God to show who had his approval. They all thought they knew: each group was convinced they were right. So there they were, all in their little groups, taking part in the Lord's Supper.

And isn't that just the kind of thing that goes on today? Someone in the church will take a stand on what he or she regards as a point of principle, and will pray piously, 'Lord, you know what these silly people round here are like: they don't know that you and I have got it right.'

The divisions in the Corinthian church stemmed from the fact that the people were full of their own importance: they were convinced they were right, and had to prove it. But Paul says, 'I know nothing by myself.' He will not even judge himself. For the day will come when God 'will make manifest the counsels of the hearts' (1 Cor. 4:4–5).

The second problem was that they did not worship at the Lord's Table together. Verses 20 and 21 of chapter 11 bring this out: 'When ye come together therefore into one place, this is not to eat the Lord's supper.' (The Greek here reads, 'It is not possible to eat the Lord's Supper.') 'For in eating everyone taketh before other his own supper: and one is hungry, and another is drunken.' As the NIV says, 'For as you eat each of you goes ahead without waiting for anybody else.'

In the early days of the Church, the Lord's Supper took the form of a 'love-feast' or common meal, which climaxed in the communion meal as we know it. However, because of their bad behaviour, the meal could not be called 'The Lord's Supper'. They might think it was the Lord's Supper, said Paul, but it was not. 'What?' he says. 'Have ye not houses to eat and to drink in?' (v.22).

The third thing the Corinthians were doing wrong was that they were abusing the Church by carrying their open divisions, even their class distinctions, right into the church. In verse 22 Paul asks, 'Despise ye the church of God, and shame them that have not?' I wonder how many Christians today have read that passage a thousand times and never noticed those words: 'them that have not'?

These Corinthian Christians were pretending to worship. They were coming in with food, and it didn't seem to bother them that there were some who didn't have anything to eat. So Paul pleaded with them not to come into the church to parade their greed, for that only emphasised their economic divisions.

And this also applies to us. If we are divided among ourselves, and eaten up by resentment and self-righteousness, then let us please stay at home, and not come to the Lord's Table. Because if we do come, we will not be worshipping properly.

At this point, Paul elucidates the true purpose and meaning of the Lord's Supper. He says in verses 23–25: 'For I have received of the Lord that which also I delivered unto you, That the Lord Jesus the same night in which he was betrayed took bread: And when he had given thanks, he brake it, and said, Take, eat: this is my body, which is broken for you: this do in remembrance of me. After the same manner also he took the cup, when he had supped, saying, This cup is the new testament in my blood: this do ye, as oft as ye drink it, in remembrance of me.'

Here Paul does something which he doesn't do many times in the New Testament. He brings in the fact that he got this teaching from Jesus himself: 'For I have received of the Lord . . .' While we know that Paul believed he got all that he said from the Lord, once in a while, for emphasis, he actually says that he did. And New Testament scholars know these verses as 'the word of the Lord sayings'. You can read one in 1 Thessalonians 4:15: 'For this we say unto you by the word of the Lord, that we which are alive and remain unto the coming of the Lord shall not prevent them which are asleep.'

Paul reserves this emphasis for very important points, which is why he uses it here. And from these verses we can discover what you might call the 'ABC' of worship at the Lord's Table. For it is amazing how we can do something for years and years and think we know so much about it, only to find suddenly that we really know so little.

The first thing we can see is that worship at the Lord's Table was initiated by Jesus Christ himself. It is the Lord's own design. So much of what we do in our church services is merely man-made tradition. In fact, one reason for this series of studies on worship is to see if we can discover what are the true spiritual elements of worship. But with the Lord's Supper there should be no confusion because if we look carefully at the New Testament teaching we find that God has told us all we need to know about its purpose and structure.

Firstly, we see, for example, that the Lord's Supper need not be a very lengthy meal, because there is just bread and wine. You don't come to the Lord's Table to get your stomach filled.

Secondly, the satisfaction we get from this table is

spiritual and not physical.

Thirdly, the meal is given in honour of Jesus Christ, and not of anyone else who may be partaking. In particular it points to his death, his resurrection and his Second Coming. Thus, in verse 26 Paul concludes: 'For as often as ye eat this bread, and drink this cup, ye do shew the Lord's death till he come.'

The second main thing we can see is that true worship at the Lord's Table only happens when certain conditions are in operation. Paul gives a series of sober exhortations, and whether or not we apply them will determine whether we will actually worship at the Lord's Table.

The first is that the eating and drinking be done in a worthy manner, because, 'Whosoever shall eat this bread, and drink this cup of the Lord, unworthily, shall be guilty of the body and blood of the Lord' (v.27). And Paul says no more on this subject at this juncture.

The second thing which must happen is that there must be self-examination. Verse 28 says: 'Let a man examine himself, and so let him eat of that bread, and drink of that cup.'

The third exhortation is that there should be a discerning of the Lord's body: 'For he that eateth and drinketh unworthily, eateth and drinketh damnation to himself, not discerning the Lord's body' (v.29).

What did Paul mean by 'unworthily'? This word has been a problem for many of us, because the criteria for 'worthiness' can easily be misunderstood, especially by people with sensitive consciences, or by the self-righteous who think they are obviously worthy.

But worthiness does not necessarily relate to our outward and moral conduct. It may do, but we can be scrupulously moral, and still be very unworthy. Worthiness is based upon our ability to discern the Lord's body. And that ability does not come from a high level of intelligence, or an extensive theological training. It comes through self-examination (v.28).

But what kind of 'examination' is it that the worshipper must pass? And what is meant by the Lord's body?

First of all, the examination. This should be both subjective and objective. Paul puts the subjective examination first. When you are being subjective, you examine yourself. And Paul, in his account of the ways the Corinthians were abusing the Lord's Table, gave them the standards against which they were to examine themselves.

Now it may be that you feel these criticisms of the Corinthians don't apply to you. Certainly these are not the only ways in which the Lord's Supper can be abused. Nevertheless, if you examine yourself, you may be surprised at how relevant they are. I have been very convicted, as I have prepared the material for this chapter, and have come to the conclusion that I myself have partaken of the Lord's Supper unworthily many times, and that God has been very merciful to me.

How, then, do we set about this subjective examination? Simply, we look at the criticisms Paul makes and ask ourselves honestly whether we ever do the same things. First, do I go about claiming that my particular views have God's stamp of approval? The invariable cause of divisions among the people of God is the claim to be right. You may claim that the church services ought to start at 10.30 am or at 11 am, or that there should be more prayer meetings, or more evangelism – and you may be right in your views. But you *don't* have to claim that you are. The great apostle Paul said, 'I don't even judge myself.' There will come a day when the secret counsels of our hearts will all be out in the open. And that will be an awful day. Then everyone will know who really had God's approval, and the more you have overclaimed, the more you will blush.

I find it quite extraordinary that Paul should say that he would not judge himself. Are we really so sure that we have God's approval? If we are, then we are claiming more even than Paul.

The second question I should ask myself is: do I take the bread and wine as if I am engaging in a private ritual between myself and Jesus alone?

Third, am I indifferent to the needs and feelings of those who are not as well off as I? Am I insensitive to others? Here were these people in the church of Corinth with their big baskets of food, and they just ate away. It didn't bother them that there were families around with very little to eat, burdened by financial worries. Instead they looked at them and said, 'These people ought to get jobs. It's their own fault if they're poor. They must be doing something wrong.'

James 2:6 says, 'But ye have despised the poor.' An individual Christian or a church with that mentality is not discerning the Lord's body. When Paul wrote to the Galatian Christians he reminded them that James, Cephas and John (with whom he had had difficulties) all agreed with him that they 'should remember the poor' (Gal. 2:10).

A church which is to have the blessing of God must be a people's church. Not a trendy church. Nor a student church. Not an elitist or a middle-class body. All the kinds of people that Jesus attracted must feel welcome.

Let these three words help us, then, with our self-examination: self-importance, self-isolation and insensitivity. We will have passed the test when we refuse to claim that we are in the right over against another Christian, when we are at peace with all our Christian brothers and sisters, and when we feel an abiding compassion for those who don't have as much as we have.

That is the subjective examination. When we have got this right, we will likely pass the objective examination, which is the examination which Jesus gives us when we face him at his coming again: our hope is in his blood.

Now I want to move on to the second question I raised, which was: 'What is actually meant by "the Lord's body"?'

Put simply, it is feeling Jesus near. It is *not* seeing physical bread and calling it Jesus. It is *not* seeing physical wine and calling it Jesus' blood. It is not even just concluding that you are saved because you are trusting in the merit of his death; although of course it includes that. But neither is it seeing the Lord's Supper merely as a memorial service. That is taking the words, 'This do in remembrance of me' too far.

Calvin got it right when he said it is 'discerning his spiritual presence'. When we partake of the bread and the wine, Jesus draws near. We know this because he said that he would be there. In Matthew 26:29 Jesus said, 'But this I say unto you, I will not drink henceforth of this fruit of the vine, until that day when I drink it new with you in my Father's kingdom.' And the kingdom of Jesus is here, now. As Christians we are members of it. So when we come to the Lord's Supper, Jesus is there. The question to ask is: 'Do we see him?'

But why does Paul say, 'the Lord's body'? It is because Jesus has a body. It wasn't only his spirit or his soul that ascended. Jesus is in his body now. The Spirit will make him real to us to the extent that our pride is swallowed up by true humility.

But, finally, what if we don't discern him? Well, there is judgment. This is the word Paul uses, although the Authorised Version says 'damnation': 'He that eateth and drinketh unworthily, eateth and drinketh damnation to himself' (v.29). This refers to temporal judgment – that is, it takes place in this life. It takes two forms (there may be others, but here Paul specifies two): God can judge us (v.32) or we can judge ourselves (v.31). Its purpose is that we should not be condemned along with the world in the final judgment (v.32). We know this will not happen to Christians – the Lord shows that Christians are his children by judging them himself and chastening them in this life (v.32).

This chastening is described in verse 30: 'For this cause

many are weak and sickly among you, and many sleep.'
Because these people in Corinth had abused the Lord's
Supper by violating the three principles I have shown
you, some of them had become ill, and some had actually
died. This was God's judgment on them.

Alternatively, we can judge ourselves in the ways I have
shown you in this chapter. Then God will say: All right,
thank you for that. Now I won't have to judge you. 'For
if we would judge ourselves, we should not be judged'
(v.31). If we confess our sins to God we relieve him of
having to judge us. He doesn't want to step in, for if he
does, it may not be so pleasant. But, 'If we confess our
sins, he is faithful and just to forgive us our sins, and to
cleanse us from all unrighteousness' (1 John 1:9).

And when we are cleansed, the ungrieved Spirit man-
ifests himself – the Lord is among us – and we worship
as we meet with him at his Table.

CHAPTER 10

THE CHURCH AT PRAYER

'And they continued stedfastly in the apostles' doctrine, and fellowship, and in breaking of bread, and in prayers.' (Acts 2:42)

Prayer can no more be divorced from worship than life can be divorced from breathing. If we follow his impulse, the Holy Spirit will always lead us to pray. When we allow him to work freely, he will always bring the Church to extensive praying. Conversely, when the Spirit is absent, we will find excuses not to pray. We may say, 'God understands. He knows I love him. But I'm tired . . . I'm so busy . . . It's just not convenient now . . .' When the Spirit is absent, our excuses always seem right, but in the presence of the Spirit our excuses fade away.

All prayer comes from the Spirit – be it disciplined prayer, or spontaneous prayer.

We pray spontaneously, both privately and with other Christians, when we are suddenly aware of a great need in the world or the Church. There are two examples of this in Acts. In chapter 12 we are told that Herod had just killed James, the brother of John, and had thrown Peter in prison. The Church was wondering just what would happen next, and we read in verse 5: 'Peter therefore was kept in prison; but prayer was made without ceasing of the church unto God for him.' This was spontaneous prayer caused by a burden for Peter.

The other example is in the passage in Acts 4 which we looked at in Chapter 8. Peter and John had been called before the Sanhedrin and had been commanded 'not to speak at all nor teach in the name of Jesus' (v.18). And when they reported this to the Church, a burden came on the people so that, 'When they heard that, they lifted up their voice to God with one accord, and said . . . now Lord, behold their threatenings' (vv.24, 29).

God often uses something external to bring the Church to her knees. We ought to see it as the kindness of God when he allows trouble to drive us to prayer. In our individual lives, family tension or financial worries or illness will do it. With the Church it can be threats – 'Behold their threatenings . . .' or fear of the future. The early Church did not know what they would do without Peter.

We also pray spontaneously when there is an overwhelming inner pressure from the Spirit resulting in a vivid awareness of the Spirit's presence. When this happens within the Church, people come from everywhere to be there. You've heard of the moral majority, and the silent majority. Here I'm talking about the sudden majority!

I've already written about the great outpouring of the Spirit that is taking place in Korea. The largest church in the world is in Seoul. Hundreds of people come every morning at five o'clock to pray before they go to work. Just imagine doing that! Yet this is what will likely happen in our churches when the ungrieved Spirit is present in power.

The people who appear from nowhere and get involved in praying will not have been toiling in prayer for months, even years, seeking God for this very outpouring of the Spirit. Yet they will derive as much benefit, if not more, as those who have been bearing the burden of prayer, and this can be a source of tension. There will be a temptation to bitterness when the faithful few see outsiders take the limelight and receive such great blessing. Do you remember the parable which Jesus told in Matthew 20 about the manager of the vineyard who hired some labourers to work all day for a penny? We are told that at the eleventh hour he found some more men who didn't have anything to do, and he hired them also to work for a penny. But when the wages were given out, those who had worked all day supposed that they would get more than the men who had come in at the eleventh hour, and they were very angry when they didn't. Well, this is what will happen when the Spirit comes. Others will come in 'at the eleventh hour' and will be blessed. As Jesus said, 'But many that are first shall be last; and the last shall be first' (Matt. 19:30).

What are the characteristics of this kind of spontaneous impulse to pray? There are four: time becomes unimportant; there is a caring for others (for example, in Acts 2:44 we are told that the believers 'had all things in common'); there is clear guidance; and there is unity (Acts 2:46 says there was 'singleness of heart').

The result of all this is – worship. We need to understand that worship is not just singing hymns, nor even consciously adoring God. Some people think that worship is limited to the moments in which one is saying, 'God, I worship you.' But this is a wrong idea. Worship is any activity which is carried out under the impulse of the Spirit of God and we are also worshipping God when we are praying for others or witnessing to others.

Arthur Blessitt tells of a church which decided to meet on a Saturday afternoon to pray for revival. About forty men came, sat in a big circle, and started to pray. The first man prayed for about five to six minutes in pious tones, with all the right phrases. The second did the same, and the third, and the fourth and the fifth. But there was no sense of the presence of God. Arthur groaned to himself and thought, 'There's something wrong here.'

At that moment he happened to look out of the

window, and noticed a restaurant across the street. He felt an impulse to get up and go over there, so he did. He stood inside the door and said, as only Arthur could say, 'Does anybody here want to get saved?'

A waitress immediately said, 'I do.'

So he went over to her, explained the gospel, and led her to the Lord.

Then he asked her how long she had been working in the restaurant, and she said, 'Two years.'

He asked her if she knew any of the people from the church across the street, and she replied, 'Oh, yes, they come here all the time, especially after the Sunday morning service.'

So he asked her if any of these people had ever talked to her about Jesus Christ, or invited her to come to church.

She said, 'No, not a one.'

Yet those same people were praying for revival.

Arthur walked back into the prayer meeting (where they had reached about the eighteenth person) and said to them, 'You can stop your praying. God has shown us what to do.'

Do not limit the Spirit by presuming that your familiar comfortable pattern of worship is the pattern he wants. Those forty men ended up praying more than ever – but first they had to be dislodged from their deadness. Worship and prayer under the impulse of the Spirit means following the Spirit.

So far I have just been speaking about spontaneous prayer. There is also what I call the disciplined impulse, the trained impulse to pray. I think this is what we particularly need to hear about today. Hebrews 5:14 says: 'But strong meat belongeth to them that are of full age, even those who by reason of use have their senses exercised to discern both good and evil.' The disciplined impulse is a developed sense of what pleases God. It is true spirituality.

Disciplined prayer arises from two things: first, a good general knowledge of God's word; second, a strong desire to please him. In other words, I am talking here about praying as an act of sheer obedience whether we feel like it or not. And it is the mature Christian who follows this way. If you think that the spontaneous impulse is the only kind that matters, you show yourself to be a superficial Christian. If you only respond to God when you are carried along by feeling, then you are an immature Christian.

Paul said to Timothy, 'Be instant in season, out of season' (2 Tim. 4:2). There are times when the spontaneous impulse is at work: this corresponds to being 'in season'; there are also times when we feel nothing: this is being 'out of season'. It is what the members of a church do when they are 'out of season' that testifies to their maturity. And it is this that demonstrates their commitment to God and each other.

Someone came to see me who said that as a result of reading one of my books, he had started to tithe. 'But,' he said, 'ever since I started I've had nothing but financial trouble. So I guess the Holy Spirit is telling me not to tithe.' But his problem was that he was not committed. When God leads us to do something we have got to do it.

You may decide to spend more time in prayer, but then you find that everything seems to militate against it. So you think, 'These things which are stopping me praying are providential.'

That's what Jonah said. He ran from God, and wanted to get a ship to Tarshish. Lo and behold – when he got to the dock, there was a ship going to Tarshish! And he said to himself, 'This is providential.' We can call any sin or temptation providential.

So don't be surprised if, when you commit yourself to prayer, everything seems to be hindering you. There must be discipline. If you live only by the spontaneous impulse to pray, you will become like the Quakers, who carry the idea of being led by the Spirit to extremes. I heard of a couple who waited for two hours for the man who was to marry them to feel moved by the Spirit to perform the ceremony. And they eventually left in tears because he never did feel moved.

One of the forgotten verses in the book of Acts is the opening verse of chapter 3. The chapter goes on to describe how Peter and John healed the crippled man, but what is interesting is that it happened when they were on their way to the temple to pray. Verse 1 says, 'Now Peter and John went up together into the temple *at the hour of prayer,* being the ninth hour.' This was three o'clock in the afternoon. So we see that even when the Spirit was present in great power, these early disciples were not afraid to go by a schedule. At this high peak in the history of the Church it would seem that the first Christians still observed set times for prayer.

The principle is that if you live by the disciplined impulse you will get the spontaneous impulse as well, and this is why I urge each Christian to pray for thirty minutes a day, and to attend the weekly church prayer meetings. Here were Peter and John on their way to the temple, when the lame beggar held out his hand to them, expecting to receive some money. But Peter just turned to him and said, 'Silver and gold have I none; but such as I have give I thee: In the name of Jesus Christ of Nazareth rise up and walk.' And the man was healed.

At the end of Luke's Gospel we are told that Jesus appeared to 'the eleven gathered together and them that were with them' (Luke 24:33), and said, 'Tarry ye in the city of Jerusalem, until ye be endued with power from on high' (v.49). On the day of Pentecost 120 people were present, and in only ten days that comparatively small number of 120 praying people gathered out of contemporary Judaism a Christian congregation of 3,000. What occurred in Acts chapter 1 was done by disciplined impulse: and they 'all continued with one accord in prayer and supplication' (v.14). What took place in Acts 2 was by spontaneous impulse: 'And they were all filled with the Holy Ghost, and began to speak with other tongues, as the Spirit gave them utterance' (v.4). And what followed? 'They continued stedfastly in the apostles' doctrine and fellowship, and in breaking of bread, and in *prayers*'. You never outgrow the need to pray.

One May evening, while I was going through my reading for the day, I came across Psalm 50, verse 12, where God says, 'If I were hungry, I would not tell thee.' And something happened to me then. That verse did more to convict me to pray than any book on prayer I have read. You may think that it has nothing to do with prayer, but this verse showed me that God will not necessarily tell us when we are doing it wrong. We may justify ourselves when we don't have time to pray, and our reasons may sound perfectly good and right to us. But God has said, 'If I were hungry, I would not tell thee.' None of us is so spiritual that we can assume that God will tap us on the shoulder and let us know every time we are doing it wrong. This convinced me that it is my job, not only as a Christian minister, but as a child of God, never to excuse myself again for what I haven't done regarding time spent in prayer.

A lot of the praying I've been talking about in this chapter is not going to take place on Sundays, but on other days of the week: when we are by ourselves, or in small groups. I long for the Christian Church to give more time to disciplined prayer. It is not always exciting, but without it, there will be no spiritual life and no worship of any kind.

CHAPTER 11

LIFESTYLE WORSHIP

'I therefore, the prisoner of the Lord, beseech you that ye walk worthy of the vocation wherewith ye are called.'
(Ephesians 4:1)

In these past chapters we have seen that worship is not a performance, or an ego trip. It is something that glorifies God and pleases him. God tells us how to worship him, and we find out, not by looking over our shoulder at what other people are doing, not by following trends, be they charismatic or anti-charismatic, but by faithful prayer, and by listening to God's word in expectancy and humility.

We have also seen that worship does not only happen on a Sunday in church, but whenever we act in obedience to the impulse of the Spirit and in his power. If an ungrieved Spirit is at work in us we will be worshipping in all we do, and we will get worship right.

This is something I want to look at more closely. What we are individually, twenty-four hours a day, is more important than what happens in church once a week. The secret of acceptable worship lies in how we are at home, or at work, and when we are alone and nobody knows what we are doing. It lies in our total lifestyle. Jesus said, 'He that is faithful in that which is least is faithful also in much' (Luke 16:10). If we don't get our act together before we come to church, we can't expect to worship at church. We can't expect something magical to happen once we're inside the church doors. We mustn't think, 'All I need to do is get to church,' because it doesn't work that way. If we are hypocrites, if our profession of faith lacks reality, when we come to church to sing and worship we will be out of tune, and will not be making music pleasing to God.

In our corporate worship it is essential to have inner – spiritual – harmony. In Ephesians 4:3 Paul speaks of 'the unity of the Spirit'. By this he means that the leadership of the Spirit in you will not contradict the leadership of the Spirit in me. If we are guided by the Spirit we will be in agreement. The ungrieved Spirit in me can detect the ungrieved Spirit in you: and there will be no heaviness when we come together – only peace and agreement.

Matthew 18:19 says: 'If two of you shall agree on earth as touching any thing that they shall ask, it shall be done for them of my Father which is in heaven.' This word which is translated 'agree' is the Greek word from which we also get the word 'symphony'. It is used like this in Acts 15:15: 'And to this agree the words of the prophets.' In Acts 5:9 it is said of Ananias and Sapphira: 'How is it that ye have agreed together to tempt the Spirit of the Lord?' 2 Corinthians 6:15 translates it as 'concord': 'What concord hath Christ with Belial?'

In a symphony orchestra all the instruments play their own parts, but according to one overall pattern, and the result is lovely music. But how did the individuals in an orchestra learn to play their instruments? If I suddenly wanted an orchestra here today, and passed out instruments among you all, would you know what to do with them?

I was an oboist in a symphony orchestra when I was in High School in Kentucky. I learned that when the conductor comes up with a piece, he wants each member to practise it during the week. So I had to take the score home with me. And how well the orchestra performed at the next rehearsal depended on how each person handled his own part.

It is the same with worship. It is not possible, for example, to go to Hyde Park Corner and say, 'I want a hundred people to stand over here – it doesn't matter whether you are a Christian or not – and we are all going to worship God.' You just don't do it like that. When we meet together to worship, God is not looking for aesthetic beauty, but for the presence of the ungrieved Spirit in each worshipping member of the congregation.

It is said that the great conductor Arturo Toscanini had such a perfect ear that he could detect if the fifth violinist on the fourth row back was slightly out of tune. Well, I don't know if it is possible for any minister to have that kind of sensitivity about his congregation. But God knows when there is perfect harmony and a lifestyle that is in accord with the Spirit – and he is not to be fooled or played around with.

The way we guard against being a hypocrite six days a week and acting piously on Sundays is by applying the word of God to our lives. Revival in a church may be quite extraordinary, but it is only a question of whether each member is following the conductor's score in his private life. In an orchestra, the sound is no greater than the sum of the different parts. As Paul says in Ephesians 4:16: 'From whom the whole body fitly joined together and compacted by that which every joint supplieth, according to the effectual working in the measure of every part, maketh increase of the body unto the edifying of itself in love.' So our worship ought to be a glorious symphony to God – no one out of tune, no one playing too loudly, each person following his or her own score.

Though our worship is not a performance designed to attract other people, or pander to our own love of display, there is a sense in which it is a performance – a performance for God. I don't know what it would be like to play for Her Majesty the Queen – but I know it is considered a great honour. If she were to go to a concert in the Royal Albert Hall, the orchestra would certainly want to play very well that day. Our worship is for God, the King of kings – should that not affect us as we prepare for the Sunday worship – since our Sunday worship is the culmination of what we are all the time?

How do we actually achieve this? How does the right performance come about? There are several ways, and, as I've indicated, the first is practice at the individual level. I don't mean that we spend the week rehearsing the following Sunday's hymns! Paul says, in Ephesians 4:1–2: 'I therefore, the prisoner of the Lord, beseech you that ye walk worthy of the vocation wherewith ye are called, with all lowliness and meekness, with longsuffering, forbearing one another in love.' This is what we must do – and practice makes perfect!

Brother Lawrence, the French monk, says in his book, *The Practice of the Presence of God*, that he felt the presence of the Lord as much among the rattling of the pots and pans in the monastery kitchen where he washed up, as when he 'bowed at the blessed sacrament'. He knew the presence of God all the time. We can all practise living in the presence of God from minute to minute. And in order to do this, we must outlaw all bitterness from our lives. We must seek to be filled with love, and with total forgiveness and acceptance of each other.

The second way a correct performance in worship is achieved is when we all discover our place in the great orchestra. Ephesians 4:7 says, 'Unto every one of us is given grace according to the measure of the gift of Christ.' Of course, there is a difference between being in an orchestra and finding our place in the body of Christ, because in an orchestra, we are the ones who choose the instrument we are going to play, but with the body, God selects our part.

The question of spiritual gifts is a subject of great

importance, and I wish to spend the next chapter considering it. However, I would like to give two general principles here, for if followed they will both have a dramatic effect on our lifestyle and go a long way to resolving the difficulties so many Christians have with this subject.

Do you wish to discover your spiritual gift? Two passages in particular tell you how to do it.

In 1 Corinthians 12:31 Paul says, 'Covet earnestly the best gifts: and yet shew I unto you a more excellent way.' In the Greek, this passage means: 'The excellent *way by which you discover* your gifts is by love.' It sounds almost too simple to be true: you can best discover your gift when you demonstrate agape love. Yet it is true. When we love people and long to serve them, when we totally forgive, and keep no record of wrongs, then we spontaneously find ways of expressing that love: and the gifts of the Spirit emerge in us. There are no short cuts to finding the gifts. We must have hearts devoid of bitterness.

The second principle is found in Romans 12. Paul says here: 'I beseech you therefore, brethren, by the mercies of God, that ye present your bodies a living sacrifice, holy, acceptable unto God, which is your reasonable service. And be ye not conformed to this world: but be ye transformed by the renewing of your mind, that ye may prove what is the good and acceptable, and perfect will of God.'

He goes on to add: 'For I say, through the grace given unto me, to every man that is among you, not to think of himself more highly than he ought to think; but to think soberly, according as God hath dealt to every man the measure of faith' (Rom. 12:1–3). Paul means: don't claim to have what you don't have.

Though, as we will see in the next chapter, we are to covet the gifts, we must not seek them for our own glory, or impute to ourselves abilities that simply aren't there. Our lives must be given over to the praise and love of God. We must live sacrificial lives, seeking at each moment only to love and serve God in holiness, humility and prayer. Then, though we may not be the first violinist or the conductor, we will quite naturally and simply find our own gift, and our place in the orchestra, almost without realising it. Sometimes we may find we are merely sweeping up, sometimes the position may be quite prominent. But it will be under God's control and God's responsibility, and almost a matter of indifference to us, since all that matters is God's glory and not ours. 'Seekest thou great things for thyself? seek them not,' said Jeremiah (45:5).

One further guideline here is that God does not encourage us to be incompetent, and if we feel that we are working incompetently, then it is a pretty strong hint that we are not where God intended us to be. We have got there by ourselves. And the indication that something is not right is that we will have stress and worry and fatigue. If you find that these are the marks of your life, ask God what he wants you to change in your life, and then offer yourself to him again as a living and daily sacrifice.

Then the third way to achieve a right performance is to accept God's verdict concerning the conductor. Ephesians 4:11 says that God 'gave some apostles; and some, prophets; and some, evangelists; and some, pastors and teachers.' Your minister has been called by God to his present work. It is a task of the utmost responsibility. We have already considered the role of preaching in worship, and I shall be going on in Chapter 13 to look at the gift of leadership. An orchestra is not better than its conductor, so if the worship of a church isn't pleasing to God, there is a sense in which the blame falls on the vicar, pastor or elder. If a congregation takes his teaching seriously and tries to follow it, and then finds it doesn't work and their soul is starved and God's Spirit is grieved, then he must be responsible.

However, the congregation must pray for their minister and seek to follow and respect his teaching. The writer to the Hebrews says, 'Remember your leaders, who spoke the word of God to you. Consider the outcome of their way of life and imitate their faith' (Heb. 13:7). And you can't do this for just an hour or two on a Sunday – it is a daily obedience and respect or it is nothing at all. For there is also a sense in which the conductor is no greater than the members of his congregation. There is a limit to what he can do, and he cannot lead unless his congregation is willing to follow him.

This takes us on to the next point: the fourth way to find the right performance is to see that the whole orchestra follows the same score. If, when the conductor announces that the music is from Mozart, the first violinist says, 'I don't feel led to play Mozart today – I'm going to play Beethoven!'; or the French horn says, 'I'm going to play Rachmaninoff,' and the trumpeter says, 'I'm into Schumann today...' it will sound rather ridiculous when the conductor starts to wave his baton.

We do not have the right merely to do our own thing. We must follow the truth, which means the Holy Scriptures. A conductor interprets the score, and a minister interprets the Scriptures. That is his job. And it is our job to follow the score, and to be governed by the teaching of the Bible each day of the week.

The mark that we are getting it right in our churches is when we see the members of the congregation growing together into maturity and Christ-likeness... Ephesians 4:11 says: 'Till we all come in the unity of the faith, and of the knowledge of the Son of God, unto a perfect man, unto the measure of the statute of the fulness of Christ.'

We will also find that there is increasing stability in our churches: 'That we henceforth be no more children, tossed to and fro, and carried about with every wind of doctrine, by the sleight of men and cunning craftiness, whereby they lie in wait to deceive' (Eph. 4:14). If truth is recognised from error, if the church members are not swayed by fashions and gimmicks – then they are worshipping by the impulse of the Spirit.

And the result will be harmony: the whole body fitly joined together. When God's people are living lives of worship; when they know their part in God's body; when no one is out of tune and there is no bitterness; when no one is trying to get attention by playing too loudly and everyone is following the word of God and the leadership God has provided – then a great symphony of worship ascends to God, the world outside marvels, and new members are added to the Church.

CHAPTER 12

SPIRITUAL GIFTS AND WORSHIP

'Having then gifts differing according to the grace that is given to us . . .' (Romans 12:6)

We are all aware that there is widespread interest in the subject of the gifts of the Spirit. Paul devotes considerable space to spiritual gifts and does so in the context of worship. I myself covet all the spiritual gifts for myself and each member of my congregation. In fact, the only justifiable covetousness in the Bible is with reference to the gifts of the Spirit! In 1 Corinthians 12:31, Paul says, 'Covet earnestly the best gifts.' God has given us carte blanche to come before him and ask for the gifts of the Spirit.

There is not one shred of biblical evidence that the gifts of the Spirit ceased in the early Church just because we now have the Bible, though this is the view of some godly people. With the deepest respect, I maintain that this is simply a theological cop-out by those who want to explain the absence of supernatural power in the Church today. Those who hold this view support their argument with 1 Corinthians 13:10: 'When that which is perfect is come, then that which is in part shall be done away.' But when Paul talks of 'that which is perfect', he is not referring to the Bible, but to love. He has just said, 'Love never faileth: but whether there be prophecies, they shall fail; whether there be tongues, they shall cease; whether there be knowledge, it shall vanish away' (v.8). And in verse 10 he is showing that the gifts of the Spirit may subside, but love goes on.

All the spiritual gifts described in 1 Corinthians 12:8–10 are available today should God be pleased to grant them. The attainment of a spiritual gift ought not to be any more unusual than the attainment of love. It is clearly our responsibility today to seek the gift of love – and it is equally our responsibility to seek the gifts of the Spirit. As we pray for revival which continues to tarry, so ought we to pray for the gifts of the Spirit. That we may not have them does not mean that we cannot have them, any more than the absence of revival proves that revival will never come.

I personally doubt that the possession of supernatural gifts is common in the western Church today. It may be that in Third World countries spiritual gifts are more frequent. I think that there is some merit to unusual claims that come from the Third World, but I don't think the gifts are widespread in Britain, even though many people are claiming to have them. Most claims to the miraculous here in Britain do not stand the test of scrutiny. And why believe the claims regarding the unverifiable gifts, such as the word of knowledge, prophecy and tongues, when the so-called miracles usually appear phony when you examine them seriously?

Is it possible that many people are attracted to the gift of tongues because they can be imitated if you try hard enough, and it's not easy to verify them? In a charismatic church in London people stayed behind for open worship after the service. A man was present who felt he would like to pray. When everyone heard him pray they took it to be an unknown tongue, and the curate, who was in the chair, gave the interpretation with words to this effect: 'Someone here is getting his last warning. You had better act. God is speaking to someone here and you had better obey.' The man who prayed the prayer just got up and walked out. He was an African and had been praying in his own language, thanking God for his goodness and mercy.

There is, however, one test that we can apply to gifts of the Spirit within a church in order to verify whether or not they are genuinely from God or just imitations. The clue is given in 1 Corinthians 14:22–25. Paul says, 'Wherefore tongues are for a sign, not to them that believe, but to them that believe not: but prophesying serveth not for them that believe not, but for them which believe. If therefore the whole church be come together into one place, and all speak with tongues, and there come in those that are unlearned, or unbelievers, will they not say that ye are mad? But if all prophesy, and there come in one that believeth not, or one unlearned, he is convinced of all, he is judged of all: and thus are the secrets of his heart made manifest; and so falling down on his face he will worship God, and report that God is in you of a truth' (1 Cor. 14:22–25).

When the gifts of prophecy and tongues are used in a church they result in conversions. When Jesus performed miracles he would say, 'Go to the priest, let him see you. Let him see that you are no longer a leper.' There was no need to over-claim and pretend. The real gifts of the Spirit will mean that the miracles will be undoubted; the healings will be undoubted – and people will be converted.

In saying this, I am trying to be as honest as I can. I do not think one can follow on from this point and say, 'I just don't believe the gifts are available.' That is an ostrich-like approach. We may not be seeing the real gifts at the moment, but this should not discourage us. We believe the Bible, which is God's infallible word, and God says, 'Covet earnestly the best gifts.' Am I to believe that this command does not apply to me? Jesus Christ is 'the same yesterday, and today, and forever' (Heb. 13:8). There is nothing to stop him pouring out the Spirit of

God in great measure should he want to do so.

We have three options. One is to forget all about the gifts of the Spirit. Another is to claim that they are everywhere, as many charismatics maintain. The third is simply to wait for the authentic gifts. That is the option I take.

I have three main observations to make based upon 1 Corinthians 12–14. The first is this: even when the gifts are undoubtedly being exercised, not all Christians have them, for Paul says, 'For the body is not one member, but many. If the foot shall say, Because I am not the hand, I am not of the body; is it therefore not of the body? And if the ear shall say, Because I am not the eye, I am not of the body; is it therefore not of the body? If the whole body were an eye, where were the hearing? If the whole were hearing, where were the smelling? But now hath God set the members every one of them in the body, as it hath pleased him' (1 Cor. 12:14–18). We all have different gifts and every gift that God has tapped us on the shoulder and given us is equally important in the body.

In our physical body, if we have a sore toe we will be miserable all day long. We can go to the doctor with an ingrown toenail and be waiting there with someone who has cancer, and someone else with a terrible heart disease. When our turn comes and the doctor says, 'What's the matter with you?' and we say, 'I've got an ingrown toenail,' we may feel stupid. We may feel we shouldn't have gone to the doctor with something so small. Yet an ingrown toenail can cause terrific pain. The smallest part of the body can affect the whole.

When we get to heaven, the recognition there will not match earthly recognition. In heaven that one who is the little toe in the body will be rewarded as much as the eye if he has been faithful in that task.

My second observation from these chapters is that even though we are encouraged to covet any true gift of the Spirit, any gift given will be by the sovereign will of God.

'But all these worketh that one and the selfsame Spirit, dividing to every man severally *as he will*' (1 Cor. 12:11). Look at verse 18: 'But now hath God set the members every one of them in the body, *as it hath pleased him*.' When it comes to the gifts of the Spirit, whether we like it or not, we are shut up to the sovereignty of God. Consequently, we must beware of the danger of working ourselves up and producing the unauthentic and phony.

Would you want God to do what he doesn't want to do? Would you want to have what God doesn't want you to have? Think of verse 15 in Psalm 106: 'He gave them their request; but sent leanness into their soul.' I don't want to be found trusting God for anything but what he wants to give to me.

When God gives a gift of the Spirit it is for two reasons. The first is for his glory. We must ask ourselves what our motive is for wanting a gift of the Spirit. What is our motive for wanting to see healings? It may be that we want to get a bit of glory for ourselves. In that case, God knows that we couldn't be trusted with these gifts. How dare we want to compete with God's glory! May we be brought to the place where we are so totally dedicated to his honour and glory that God can trust us with the unusual. The withholding of God's gifts suggests that our motives are wrong.

The second reason he gives a gift is for the edification of others: 'Even so ye, forasmuch as ye are zealous of spiritual gifts, seek that ye may excel to the edifying of the church' (1 Cor. 14:12). God gives gifts so that we may be givers.

Do you know what may well be the greatest gift of the Spirit? It is described in 1 Corinthians 12. Most of us have heard of the gifts of knowledge, of faith, of miracles, of tongues. We have heard of the gift of the interpretation of tongues. But how many know about the gifts of *helps*? 'God hath set some in the church, first apostles, secondarily prophets, thirdly teachers, after that miracles, then gifts of healings, helps . . .' (v.28).

Someone may say, 'Help! I've only got the gift of helps!' Maybe your church needs cleaning and you are the one gifted to do it. Or somebody is needed to help in the kitchen. Stewards, musicians, typists, Sunday school helpers, people who go out witnessing, or help run meetings and organisations, consistent tithers – these people should be doing this work with the God-given gift of help. Some can only do one thing. Some can do three or four things without fatigue. The body will never be tired and no one will be overworked when we all do our part. If someone is the little toe and works well, that person will see that the body goes on without any pain.

A man may be praying for the gift of healing and be blind to the fact that he has a gift – to help make coffee. How sad for him that he doesn't see it. Maybe by ignoring this gift he is blocking the way for the gift of healing.

As far as I am able to tell, spiritual gifts emerge in one of two ways. First, it may be your natural gift plus the Spirit. God had a purpose in making each of us as we are. We are each unique and each have a place in his kingdom. What we can do naturally, that is, what we would have even if we hadn't been converted, can be improved and controlled by the Spirit.

Secondly there are the supernatural gifts of the Spirit such as miracles and healing. We aren't born with these gifts. To perform a miracle, to heal, is something God does. But it wouldn't surprise me for one minute if God were graciously to overrule so that the one who does the cleaning or catering is also the one who is able to lay hands on somebody and see a supernatural healing, or be given a special gift of prayer and discernment.

My third observation about 1 Corinthians 12 and 14 is that Paul gives clear instructions about how to go about obtaining the gifts. I have already touched on this in Chapter 11, but I would like to return to it. I found it thrilling when I first understood that when Paul said in

1 Corinthians 12:31: 'Covet earnestly the best gifts: and yet shew I unto you a more excellent way,' that Paul was showing us *how to get the gifts*. The way to get them is by the love of 1 Corinthians 13.

One of the treasured moments of my life came some years ago when I went to Holland and was given the very high privilege of meeting Corrie ten Boom in her home. I asked her, 'Is it true that you believe in all the gifts of the Spirit?'

'Oh, yes,' she said. '1 Corinthians 12, 1 Corinthians 14, but don't forget 1 Corinthians 13.'

Paul is saying, 'The Spirit is released to be himself to the degree that we have *agape* love.' It is not by fantasising about the gifts. It is not even by praying for them, much less coveting them. Here is the way: it is by love. The bridge that crosses the gap between the sovereignty of God and the obtaining of spiritual gifts is love.

Those of us who long for the gifts of the Spirit for our own lives and for our church worship – not the phony gifts not the counterfeits, but the true gifts – need to apply ourselves to a number of principles from 1 Corinthians 13.

First, the love of 1 Corinthians 13 tolerates those who seem inferior. Paul says, 'Love suffereth long, and is kind' (v.4). They may seem inferior socially, or culturally or intellectually. They may seem inferior spiritually. But you are kind and you suffer them long.

Secondly, this love is content with the present circumstances. Paul says, 'Love envieth not' (v.4). This is very important. James said that we should be 'perfect and entire, wanting nothing' (James 1:4). 'The Lord is my Shepherd; I shall not want,' says David (Ps. 23:1). We must come to the place where we say, 'I have all that God wants me to have materially right now.' Love does not envy.

Thirdly, love doesn't want to make another person jealous. Paul says, 'Love vaunteth not itself, is not puffed up' (v.4). That means it doesn't boast. Do you know why people boast? It is partly because of their insecurity, but it is mainly because they want to be admired. At bottom, they want to make you just a bit jealous by revealing who they know, what they know, or what they have. But love protects another person from being envious.

The fourth thing is that this love is never rude: love 'doth not behave itself unseemly' (v.5). Fifth, love doesn't manipulate either people or progress. Paul says that it 'seeketh not her own' (v.5). The NIV puts it: 'Not self-seeking.' Sixth, it doesn't exhibit a quick temper: 'not easily provoked' (v.5). When this love sees any form of bitterness emerging on the horizon it just refuses to give place to the devil. It also 'thinketh no evil' (v.5): 'keeps no record of wrongs' (NIV). That is the way God forgives us. The blood of Jesus washes away all our sins. It is as though we never committed them. That is what love is. Paul says we should be 'forgiving one another, even as God for Christ's sake hath forgiven us' (Eph. 4:32). If a person has hurt us, or walked over us, or been unkind to us, we don't even know about it.

All this is pretty hard. Do we want the gifts of the Spirit or have we changed our minds? Today there is an absence of the gifts of the Spirit in the Church, not because they ceased with the early Church, but because we all want short cuts. Paul says, 'Covet earnestly the best gifts,' and here is how to get them. We have forgotten 1 Corinthians 13, and that is why revival tarries, and there is so much that is phony.

If a man or woman came to know this kind of love which keeps no record of wrong, knows no bitterness, doesn't want to make another person envious, isn't proud, tolerates others, is gracious and kind and doesn't envy, it may be that he or she will wake up one day and find that God has entrusted him or her with a valuable gift that is more precious than the knowledge of a brain surgeon or the skill of the cleverest barrister in the city.

Such a person may say, 'I can't believe it would happen to me.'

But God has done this because love bridges the gap between the sovereignty of God and the obtaining of the gifts. How dare we talk about the gifts and treat love with contempt! If this love were to flow among us, who knows what God might do?

CHAPTER 13

LEADERSHIP IN WORSHIP

'And looking upon Jesus as he walked, he [John] saith, Behold the Lamb of God!' (John 1:36)

In this chapter I would like to concentrate on one particular and vital gift of the Spirit – the gift of leadership. From earliest times people have needed leadership because most people are followers. And it is no disgrace to be a follower: we are all followers of Jesus. Those who are upset because they are not called to be leaders in the Church are criticising the way God made them. Everybody can be a leader in some area, but once outside their area, they must have the grace to become followers again.

It is a sad day when God hides his face from the Church and does not raise up strong leadership. For when that happens, you have a lot of small men scrambling for power, and it is a pitiful sight. I don't understand why God sometimes does not provide strong leaders – why many generations have suffered because of this problem. One of the curious quirks (if I may put it like this) in Church history is the story of George Whitefield and John Wesley. Here were two great men; but only one of them was a leader. Whitefield was given over entirely to preaching and Wesley was the leader of men. Wesley organised many of Whitefield's converts, and Methodism took a certain theological complexion because of Wesley's influence.

In the Welsh Revival there was no equivalent to John Wesley. The name Evan Roberts is associated with the Revival, but he was no leader. No real leadership or definite theological direction emerged from the Welsh Revival, so that, although the churches were filled for a while, when it was over, all that was left were memories.

And many churches today flounder as a consequence of an absence of able leadership. This is a day when the so-called 'one-man ministry' is severely criticised. But I have long had a suspicion that the modern craze for 'plurality of elders', as it is termed, has its base, not in the fact that suddenly everyone has seen the light on the teaching of elders, as in a lack of leadership. And so this practice has largely come in to fill the vacuum.

Any era where God does not raise up strong leadership is tragic. If you want to know what the Book of Judges is all about, look at its very last verse: 'In those days there was no king in Israel: every man did that which was right in his own eyes.'

Moses, the greatest leader of men that ever was, had a successor in Joshua. But no one succeeded Joshua. Elijah's mantle fell on Elisha, but Elisha had no successor. And I don't understand this.

One of the main tasks of a leader in the Church is to lead the worship. Obviously a leader has other responsibilities too. He must be an administrator, and be able to delegate authority to those who respect him enough to follow him. He must be able to give direction and set the pace spiritually and theologically – 'Where there is no vision, the people perish' (Prov. 29:18).

However, since in this book my subject is worship, I should like to concentrate on leadership in worship. It could be said that Moses' main calling was to lead worship. God came to him and said: 'And they shall hearken to thy voice: and thou shalt come, thou and the elders of Israel, unto the king of Egypt, and ye shall say unto him, The Lord God of the Hebrews hath met with us: and now let us go, we beseech thee, three days' journey into the wilderness, that we may sacrifice to the Lord our God' (Exod. 3:18).

This theme comes up again and again. Exodus 7:16 says: 'And thou shalt say unto him, The Lord God of the Hebrews hath sent me unto thee, saying, Let my people go, that they may serve me in the wilderness.' The NIV translates it, 'That they may worship me in the desert.' Exodus 8:1 has: 'And the Lord spake unto Moses, Go unto Pharaoh, and say unto him, Thus saith the Lord, Let my people go, that they may serve me.'

Moses was raised up to lead the people to worship God. By 'lead worship' I don't just mean 'conduct worship' for it doesn't take a lot to do that. I fear that there are probably hundreds of unregenerate men 'conducting worship' today. What I mean by 'lead worship', is lead the congregation to worship and adore God.

There are two important things to remember about leadership in worship. The first is that the leader himself must get out of the way. The best example of someone who did this is not Moses, or Samuel, or King David – who can certainly teach us a lot about leadership in worship. It isn't even the apostle Paul. It is John the Baptist.

We know that John was called by God to be a leader. He was filled with the Holy Spirit from his mother's womb. He was part of God's plan. Matthew 3:3 says, 'For this is he that was spoken of by the prophet Esaias, saying, The voice of one crying in the wilderness, Prepare ye the way of the Lord, make his paths straight.' God trained and prepared John for leadership. It is easy to forget that John the Baptist was the son of a priest. When you think of John you get the image almost of a wild man in the desert. But he was brought up in the cultured home of a priest and he would have known all about the ritual of worship in Israel.

God also protected and guided him. We know that John was 'in the deserts till the day of his shewing unto

Israel' (Luke 1:80). He stayed put until his time had come.

John's was a preaching leadership – 'In those days came John the Baptist, preaching in the wilderness of Judaea' (Matt. 3:1). His preaching was passionate: 'But when he saw many of the Pharisees and Sadducees come to his baptism, he said unto them, 'O generation of vipers, who hath warned you to flee from the wrath to come?' (Matt. 3:7). Imagine calling these members of his congregation, snakes!

But his preaching was also practical and down-to-earth: 'Bring forth therefore fruits meet for repentance' (Matt. 3:8). And it was popular: 'Then went out to him Jerusalem, and all Judaea, and all the region round about Jordan' (Matt. 3:5). It was also effective: 'And were baptised of him in Jordan, confessing their sins' (Matt. 3:6).

Finally, his leadership was prescribed. He was a leader under authority. John didn't arbitrarily decide what to say: he was following a script. God told him what to say. And his major task was to get out of the way as soon as possible: 'He [Jesus] must increase, and I must decrease' (John 3:30). John's mission – which should be the mission of every preacher – was to prepare the people to look in one direction. In fact, you could say it was to do two things: to prepare and to direct. The preparation was to bring his hearers to the point of repentance – to 'bring forth ... fruits meet for repentance' (Matt. 3:8). The direction was to point to a person – 'The next day John seeth Jesus coming unto him, and saith, Behold the Lamb of God, which taketh away the sin of the world. This is he of whom I said, After me cometh a man which is preferred before me: for he was before me' (John 1:29–30).

The task of leadership in worship is to prepare a people and point to a person. The person is the pre-existent, eternal Son of God. We must all be brought to the point where we adore Jesus. The burden of my heart for my own church, is that as a consequence of the worship there (and I refer to the whole service) the members of the congregation will leave with a passionate love of Jesus and desire to adore him. And to do this, I as a leader must diminish.

The second thing to remember about leadership in worship is that the leader should see and follow the Spirit. The only leadership which is able to lead people out in worship and love of Jesus is leadership which is itself under the guidance of the Holy Spirit. Jesus said, 'God is a Spirit: and they that worship him must worship him in spirit and in truth' (John 4:24).

John 1:32 is a very interesting verse: 'And John bare record, saying, I saw the Spirit descending from heaven like a dove . . .' The one who wants to lead worship by the Spirit must first discern the Spirit himself. Paul said to Timothy, 'The husbandman that laboureth must be first partaker of the fruits' (2 Tim. 2:6).

The tragedy of today's generation is that most of its leaders are merely followers. They watch which way the people are going, and then jump out in front and say, 'Follow me.' They are just like the politicians who hire Mr Gallup to find out what the people are thinking. But for leadership in worship it is necessary to see the Spirit, and the only one who can see the Spirit is the person who is already filled with the Spirit.

One of the worst things that can happen to a church is to have a leader who is not a man of God, for then the worship will be a noise and a show.

'So,' someone may say, 'how can we know that our leader sees the Spirit?'

Well, the test is to see where he leads you. John 1:32 says, 'I saw the Spirit descending from heaven like a dove, and it abode upon him.' With what result? John released his followers to follow Jesus: 'Again the next day after John stood, and two of his disciples; and looking upon Jesus as he walked, he saith, Behold the Lamb of God! And the two disciples heard him speak, and they followed

Jesus' (John 1:35–37).

The leader of a church is led by the Spirit when the members of his church fall in love with the Lord Jesus Christ.

Young believers need milk at first, but then they have to be weaned. Just as growing children and adults need meat, so Christians must learn to think for themselves. It is only a selfish parent who wants to hold on to a child for ever. Leadership in worship must be a leadership that keeps out of the way as much as possible, and enables the people to see and follow Jesus in the power of the Holy Spirit.

CHAPTER 14

LEARNING FROM ANGELS

'And one cried unto another, and said, Holy, holy, holy, is the Lord of hosts.' (Isaiah 6:3)

The most perfect worshippers of God in all his creation inside or outside the universe are the angels. Presumably when we, the redeemed, are glorified, we will be able to worship God perfectly too; because in heaven we will, as Robert Murray M'Cheyne put it: 'Love God with un-sinning hearts.' But in the meantime our worship is imperfect, so surely we can learn from angels.

Angels are created, non-material, spiritual beings who cannot be seen with the naked eye unless they choose to reveal themselves to us. There are various categories of angels: cherubim, seraphim, messengers (the Greek word, *angellos*, which we translate as 'angel' means 'messenger'), principalities and powers. We know the names of two prominent angels: Michael and Gabriel, but it wouldn't surprise me to learn that every angel has his own name.

There are two orders of angels: fallen angels and unfallen angels. Jude 6 refers to those angels 'which kept not their first estate, but left their own habitation', and says that God has reserved them 'in everlasting chains under darkness unto the judgment of the great day'. According to Peter in 2 Peter 2:4, they are cast down to hell. Here the word 'hell' is the Authorised Version's translation of the Greek word *tartarus*. But we don't, in fact, know what *tartarus* means. It is not used anywhere else in the Bible, and the Authorised Version is probably wrong to translate it as hell. The word probably refers to the sphere of God's creation, which we have not yet seen, where fallen angels exist.

C. S. Lewis suggests that there is a hierarchy among the fallen angels. Satan is their commander-in-chief, and they are classed as evil spirits, devils, and demons.

The unfallen angels are those who did not give in to Satan's rebellion. It would seem that they are the elect angels, who Paul refers to in 1 Timothy 5:21, and who, according to the writer of the Hebrews are: 'all ministering spirits, sent forth to minister for them who shall be heirs of salvation' (Heb. 1:14).

There is some hint in the Bible that the angels want to learn from us. 1 Peter 1:10, 12 says, 'Of which salvation the prophets have inquired and searched diligently . . . Unto whom it was revealed, that not unto themselves, but unto us they did minister the things, which are now reported unto you by them that have preached the gospel unto you with the Holy Ghost sent down from heaven; *which things the angels desire to look into.*'

I confess that I have never understood this verse, though I have read a lot of speculation about it, perhaps not all of it unprofitable. We can say this: the angels know nothing of the joy of being redeemed.

Many years ago Oswald Smith wrote a great song, the refrain of which ran:

Holy, holy, holy is what the angels sing,
And I expect to help there, the courts of heaven ring.
But when I sing redemption's story, they will fold their wings,
For angels never felt the joy that our salvation brings.

And according to Joseph Ton, our testimony in the world matters also because of onlooking angels. Our obedience in trial, suffering or persecution is important because angels are witnessing our faithfulness.

On many occasions angels have sustained and protected God's people. Psalm 34:7 says, 'The angel of the Lord encampeth round about them that fear him, and delivereth them.' And in Psalm 91:11 we read, 'He shall give his angels charge over thee, to keep thee in all thy ways.' Now exactly when God despatches an angel, or angels, to come to our side, I do not know. Perhaps it is only in a time of trial. Or maybe at the time of our conversion an angel immediately comes alongside us and remains with us, which I believe to be the case.

Hebrews 1:14 says that angels are '. . . ministering spirits, sent forth to minister for them who *shall* be heirs of salvation'. So it could be that an angel stands guard over God's elect from the moment of their birth. But whatever the case may be, always keep in mind that your angel has had tremendous experience in fighting the devil.

Although they know nothing of the joy of redemption, angels have resisted Satan's revolt and have therefore first-hand knowledge of how to resist the devil. For you can be sure that when Satan conspired to rebel, he tried to enlist every angel in heaven. And he succeeded with some. But those who did not acquiesce know how to withstand him. So we should be able to learn from them by virtue of this fact alone.

We are dealing here with a delicate mystery, because it is difficult to tell the difference between the function of angels and the work of the Holy Spirit. I can't see, humanly speaking, why there should be any need for angels. Surely the third person of the Trinity, who is the omnipotent, omniscient, omnipresent God, could accomplish anything angels are called upon to do? But God has chosen to employ angels.

The first thing we can learn about angels with reference to worship is that angels adore God alone. The prophet Isaiah was given to see with his spiritual eyes what is going on in heaven all the time. (And I cannot deny feeling envious of Isaiah!) He says, 'In the year that King Uzziah died I saw also the Lord sitting upon a throne, high and lifted up, and his train filled the temple. Above it stood the seraphims: each one had six wings; with twain he covered his face, and with twain he covered his feet, and with twain he did fly. And one cried unto another, and said, Holy, holy, holy, is the Lord of hosts: the whole earth is full of his glory' (Is. 6:1–3).

Everything is done out of love for God. Whatever feeling angels may have for us, their priority is the glory of God. The angel standing over you is on God's side. He is a messenger, and he is for you, but he adores God alone. And nothing will ever divert him from that loyalty.

The second thing is that angels refuse to be worshipped. When John was given his glorious revelation on the Isle of Patmos, he fell at the feet of the angel. And I have always been surprised at this. You would have thought that John, 'the disciple whom Jesus loved', who 'leaned on his breast' (John 21:20), who had had a lifetime's experience of God, would have known better. But Revelation 19:10 says, 'And I fell at his feet to worship him. And he said unto me, See thou do it not: I am thy fellowservant, and of thy brethren that have the testimony of Jesus: worship God: for the testimony of Jesus is the spirit of prophecy.'

And if this were not enough, John went on to make the same mistake again. In chapter 22:8 we read: 'And I John saw these things, and heard them. And when I had heard and seen I fell down to worship before the feet of the angel which shewed me these things.' And he got the same reaction: 'Then saith he unto me, See thou do it not: for I am thy fellowservant, and of thy brethren the prophets, and of them which keep the sayings of this book: worship God' (v.9).

This teaches us not to be impatient with people who give in to idolatry or do things we don't approve of, and also that the greatest service we can perform is to direct men to God. The angel did not want any recognition or worship. He pointed to Christ – and in that he was like the Holy Spirit. We must always seek to encourage others to worship God. It never does any good to let people admire us too much, as sooner or later we will disillusion them.

When Paul wrote to the church at Corinth he had to acknowledge that there were arguments among them. For the people were saying, 'I am of Paul; and I of Apollos; and I of Cephas; and I of Christ' (1 Cor. 1:12). So Paul said to them, 'Who then is Paul, and who is Apollos, but ministers by whom ye believed, even as the Lord gave to every man? I have planted, Apollos watered; but God gave the increase. So then neither is he that planteth any thing, neither he that watereth; but God that giveth the increase' (1 Cor. 3:5–7). We must release others to worship God. And we must not follow any Christian leader uncritically, for we will have to stand before God on our own some day.

Thirdly, angels exist to do God's will. As we have seen, they are God's messengers to us, and they reveal God's will to us. This is why an angel sometimes has to do something that hurts us. When Zachariah, the father of John the Baptist, did not believe what the angel Gabriel told him, Gabriel said to him, 'Behold, thou shalt be dumb, and not able to speak, until the day that these things shall be performed, because thou believest not my words, which shall be fulfilled in their season' (Luke 1:20). And at once Zachariah was unable to speak. You can't argue or bargain with an angel: they do what they are ordered to do.

In his story of the rich man and Lazarus, Jesus said that when Lazarus died he was 'carried by the angels into

Abraham's bosom' (Luke 16:22). And it is also the awful truth that angels will escort the lost to their eternal doom. We can learn from this that we must never become so involved with people – even our closest friends – that we risk being influenced by them. We are to obey God alone.

Perfect worship of God consists of doing his will. The depth of our worship is not revealed by how high we raise our hands or how high we jump when we get excited. We worship perfectly when we obey God.

A fourth thing we may learn is that angels never tire of worshipping God. Revelation 4:8, although not a reference to angels, shows us what kind of worship there is in heaven. This verse says of the four beasts, 'They rest not day and night, saying, Holy, holy, holy, Lord God Almighty.' Throughout many thousands of years, ever since they were created, the angels have been worshipping God. And they have never tired of it, or let their worship become commonplace. And we too will experience the highest joy throughout eternity in the sheer adoration and worship of God.

Fifthly, we can see that angels worship the Lord Jesus Christ. The focal point of the worship of angels is the triune God. Now God is in three persons – *persona,* to use Tertullian's Latin word – God the Father, the Son and the Holy Spirit. Jesus, the Son, the second person of the Trinity, is eternal, and I have no doubt that the angels worshipped him as the eternal Logos – the Word – before he was made flesh in Bethlehem. Hebrews 1:6 says, 'When he bringeth in the first begotten into the world, he saith, And let all the angels of God worship him.' The angels, therefore, worshipped Jesus when he came, as the God-man, into the world.

They worship him though they do not know the joy of redemption. They know nothing of the shed blood of the cross being applied to them. How much more ought we to worship the Lord Jesus Christ, we, who were lost, hell-bound and hell-deserving, but who have been rescued because Jesus took upon himself the punishment that we deserve, and died on a cross? How much more should we fall on our faces and adore him?

And another thing about angels is that they perceive the true essence of God's character. 'And one cried unto another, and said, Holy, holy, holy, is the Lord of hosts' (Is. 6:3). They know that God is holy. How do you define holiness? One theologian has described it as 'the other-ness of God'. I think he meant that even if there were no such thing as sin, God would be still totally 'other'. God will never cease to be God throughout eternity; he will never cease to be independent of both created and redeemed beings.

So the seraphim, who don't even know what sin is, actually cover their faces with their wings in the presence of God. Isaiah says of them: 'Each one had six wings; and with twain he covered his face, and with twain he covered his feet, and with twain he did fly.' And they praise God for his essential nature. What would the sight of a holy God do to us, who are sinners? It could only have the effect of making us say, with Isaiah, 'Woe is me! for I am undone; because I am a man of unclean lips, and I dwell in the midst of a people of unclean lips for mine eyes have seen the King, the Lord of hosts' (Is. 6:5).

Moreover, even though they have been in his presence and have been worshipping him for millions of years, the angels still show great reverence for God. Humanly speaking, once we get to know a person whom we have previously only seen from afar, we lose a bit of the awe we had of them. But with God, the closer you get to him, and the better you know him, the more reverence you feel for him.

We see from Isaiah 6:3 that the angels talk to one another about God: 'And one cried unto another, and said, Holy, holy, holy, is the Lord of Hosts.' And their conversation reveals great wonder and reverence. Never let us be flippant or familiar when we talk of God or to

God. If we are superficial or off-hand, we reveal merely how far we are from God and true worship.

I wish with all my heart that Christians would talk to one another about God. We talk about the weather, about sports, about our work, about television programmes, about other people and what is happening to them, yet how strangely silent we are about God, even after the church services! Surely this is one of the greatest of all indications that our lives are empty of God, and we know nothing of true worship? 'Out of the abundance of the heart the mouth speaketh,' said Jesus (Matt. 12:35). And if our mouths are silent about God in our day to day conversation, what does that say about our hearts?

The next thing we can learn from angels is that they also perceive the extent of God's glory in the universe. Isaiah 6:3 says, '. . . the whole earth is full of his glory.' The angels see God's glory everywhere. And the reason is that angels can see the physical and the spiritual simultaneously. We are limited to what is tangible and material. But angels can see everything.

Remember what Elisha said in 2 Kings 6:16? He looked around and saw armies on every side, and his servant was scared to death. It didn't seem as if they had a chance. But Elisha said, 'Fear not: for they that be with us are more than they that be with them. And Elisha prayed, and said, Lord, I pray thee, open his eyes, that he may see. And the Lord opened the eyes of the young man; and he saw: and, behold, the mountain was full of horses and chariots of fire round about Elisha.'

The angels can see what is there, and if we could too, we would face a thousand worlds. Our worship should leave us with tremendous confidence, for in the battles we fight 'they that be with us are more than they that be with them'. Our enemy is God's enemy. And God's glory is not just in heaven but in all the earth.

And as we have already seen, angels know how to resist the devil. They have great experience in resisting him, and they do it properly. In Jude 9 we read, 'Yet Michael the archangel, when contending with the devil he disputed about the body of Moses, durst not bring against him a railing accusation, but said, The Lord rebuke thee.'

The archangel Michael did not take Satan on himself. He showed contempt for him and said, 'The Lord rebuke thee.' Don't let us ever be stupid enough to think we can take the devil on alone. Like the angels, we must say, 'The Lord rebuke you.' If they can do it, how much more should we be able to, who have the blood of Jesus as our covering?

And finally, we learn that the angels rejoice in the conversion of the lost. Jesus says, 'Likewise, I say unto you, there is joy in the presence of the angels of God over one sinner that repenteth' (Luke 15:10). And so we too should rejoice. We should not be like the brother of the prodigal son, who felt that he had not been treated well. Instead, we ought to say with his father, 'It was meet that we should make merry and be glad: for this thy brother was dead, and is alive again; and was lost, and is found' (Luke 15:32).

That is the right way to look at anybody who has come to Christ. And the fact that the angels rejoice shows what they must think of evangelism and our going out to save the lost: they are with us.

We can learn from angels. And the more we learn the better we will worship God, and the more they will rejoice. Have you ever thought that when we meet with other Christians to worship God, our angels meet together too? The more we worship, the more they rejoice. If we could only see the expression on their faces, we would know if we were getting our worship right. For that is what we are after – to become true worshippers, so that the glory of God may be acknowledged on earth as in heaven.

CHAPTER 15

SPIRITUAL WARFARE IN WORSHIP

'For we wrestle not against flesh and blood, but against principalities, against powers . . . against spiritual wickedness in high places.' (Ephesians 6:12)

In Chapter 14 we saw that there are two types of angels – fallen and unfallen. I want now to focus on fallen angels – fallen angels who are very much alive, as we see from Paul's words to the Ephesians above. Rarely have I experienced such opposition and conflict as when I was preparing the material for this chapter – which is a fairly strong hint that Satan doesn't like any effort on our part to unmask him. It also shows how threatened Satan is by worship. The devil is described in a number of ways in Scripture, for example, 'the god of this world' (2 Cor. 4:4); 'the prince of the power of the air' (Eph. 2:2); 'a roaring lion' (1 Pet. 5:8); 'the accuser of our brethren' (Rev. 12:10).

The problem of evil is unsolvable this side of heaven. We just don't know why God allowed evil to come into the world. And the Scriptures are not as clear as we would perhaps like them to be on the subject of the origin of Satan. Theologians have pieced some of the scriptures together and drawn from them a few conclusions which, as far as I know, cannot be disproved. What we believe to be true is that Satan was known as Lucifer, and that he fell, taking a number of angels with him. Isaiah 14:12 says, 'How art thou fallen from heaven, O Lucifer, son of the morning!' Jude refers to 'the angels which kept not their first estate' (v.6), and 2 Peter 2:4 says, 'God spared not the angels that sinned, but cast them down to hell . . .'

Some have speculated, from Revelation 12:4 – 'And his tail drew the third part of the stars of heaven, and did cast them to the earth' – that Satan took a third of the angels with him. And Augustine speculated that the number of God's elect will be the same as the number of angels who sinned.

Exactly what happened when evil emerged, and why God allowed it, we just don't know and trying to figure it all out is unprofitable speculation. If we understood everything, then there would be no need for faith.

What is not speculation is this: our greatest enemy is Satan, who is also the greatest enemy of Christ. What is also not speculation is that Satan's doom is already mapped out. It is described in Revelation 20:10: 'And the devil that deceived them was cast into the lake of fire and brimstone, where the beast and the false prophet are, and shall be tormented day and night for ever and ever.'

Satan already knows that this is his doom, and he is also aware that his time is limited. Revelation 12:12 says, 'Woe to the inhabiters of the earth and of the sea! for the devil is come down unto you, having great wrath, because he knoweth that he hath but a short time.' And this is one reason why he is so angry.

Something else that is certain about Satan is that he will try to take everybody down with him. I read in the paper about a man who, when he discovered that he had AIDS, tried to spread it to as many people as he could. 'If I'm going to die,' he said, 'I want others to die too.' And that's like Satan. He wants to take everybody with him.

He tries to do this by keeping people from being saved. He is called 'the god of this world' who blinds 'the minds of them which believe not, lest the light of the glorious gospel of Christ, who is the image of God, should shine unto them' (2 Cor. 4:4). Whenever anybody is not saved it shows that Satan has succeeded with them.

When Satan fails, and people are converted, he then does all that he can to keep them from holiness.He will try to get them to grieve and quench the Spirit, because he wants to keep them from a state of blissful worship.

New Christians need to be taught these things. They also need to know that the devil will attempt to push us to extreme views about him. He will either try to get us to be over-preoccupied with him, or to disregard him completely. If we become preoccupied with the occult, with witchcraft, even if it is on the grounds that we just want to learn more about the dangers of Satan, we open ourselves up to oppression, if not possession, by evil spirits. So we need to be very careful. At the other extreme, if Satan can get us to discount as rubbish anything to do with the occult, he will be very pleased because then we will fail to be on our guard.

Here are nine more things about the devil: he is jealous, insecure, vengeful and persistent. He is also unteachable (he never learns from his mistakes); a liar and a deceiver, and he is full of hate. But, most of all, he is resistible.

As I grew up, my father used to say to me, 'Son, remember that the devil is crafty. He is second only to God in power and wisdom.' And that is absolutely true. The devil is second only to God: but he is *second*, and that is why he is resistible. As Peter put it: '. . . Whom resist stedfast in the faith' (1 Pet. 5:9).

'Resist the devil, and he will flee from you,' said James (James 4:7). That is a promise, and it works!

Because of his jealousy, Satan cannot tolerate Jesus being exalted. A film star may hate hearing a rival being praised or getting good reviews. Similarly, Satan hates Jesus being exalted; he cannot bear to hear the truth preached or to see a united church where the Spirit is ungrieved and unbound.

Thus all our efforts to get our worship right will make him angry. We need to be aware of how he works and know how to combat him. His strategy is to devour, deceive and demoralise. Peter wrote: 'Be sober, be vigilant; because your adversary the devil, as a roaring lion, walketh about, seeking whom he may devour' (1 Pet. 5:8). He devours the work of God, and if he can he will abort it before it has a chance to work. He is therefore always in at the beginning: 'And the dragon stood before the woman which was ready to be delivered, for to devour her child as soon as it was born' (Rev. 12:4).Satan doesn't wait around for something to get started to see if it is going to be a threat to him. He already knows whether it will be or not, and he's in there right at the beginning.

I've already written in Chapter 7 about the importance of expectancy before worship. As we come to worship we should be undisturbed in our heart and spirit – for our preparation for worship will often be the object of Satan's attacks. Because he does not like the idea of a lot of people, all of whom enjoy the ungrieved Spirit, coming together, he will do anything that he can to disturb us just before the service. Have you ever noticed how Satan will attack you on a Sunday morning? Someone oversleeps and isn't ready. The toast is burnt and the coffee spilled. Or just as you are going out of the door you can't find the keys! And if you finally make it to church, you find that somebody is there you didn't want to see. Or perhaps someone doesn't speak to you, or doesn't smile at you as you are coming in at the door, and the whole service is ruined for you, while you wonder what you can have done to them.

This is the devil. The first time we started singing choruses in Westminster Chapel, about a dozen uninvited people came out and danced, including a sexy young lady in a mini-skirt. This produced a shocked reaction. What the devil was trying to do, I believe, was to frighten us off, but I knew we had to persist, both in our new emphasis on evangelism and in livelier worship. That's the way the devil works, wasting no time in trying to destroy the work of the Spirit. Jonathan Edwards used to say, 'Remember when the Church is revived, the devil is also revived.'

Satan goes for new converts, trying to stop any kind of follow-up; and he attacks people who make a fresh commitment by trying to stop them acting on what they have been shown. For example, when people pray about tithing, the devil is likely to bring to their minds every excuse for not tithing. Similarly, he will try to discourage those who are considering getting involved in evangelism – putting thoughts in their minds such as: 'It's not my personality . . .' 'It's too cold . . .' 'Maybe later . . .'

Satan will try to devour the whole of our worship, too. One way is by trying to push us into extreme positions; for example, he persuades us to opt for stilted singing or for complete chaos; for deathlike silence or empty noise; for teaching at the expense of singing, or vice versa.

Sometimes he tries to destroy our worship simply by trying to make us lose our concentration. He will try to draw our attention to everything under the sun in order to get our minds to wander. Often, when we have decided to spend time in prayer, we begin to think of things we must do, and before we know it, the time has gone, and we need to do something else. Secondly, Satan is out to deceive. Revelation 12:9 describes him as '...that old serpent, called the Devil, and Satan, which deceiveth the whole world'.

How does he set about his deception? In 2 Corinthians 11:14, Satan is called 'an angel of light': which means that he uses apparently respectable means and people to deceive us. He tries, firstly, to lure us away from 'the simplicity that is in Christ'. As 2 Corinthians 11:3 says, 'But I fear, lest by any means, as the serpent beguiled Eve through his subtilty, so your minds should be corrupted from the simplicity that is in Christ.'

Simplicity in worship may be one of his targets. He may get people involved in intellectual, formal types of worship which are a long way from the spirit of true worship.

Or he tries to lure us away from the truth and towards the counterfeit. Paul says: 'For if he that cometh preacheth another Jesus, whom we have not preached, or if ye receive another spirit, which ye have not received, or another gospel, which ye have not accepted, ye might well bear with him' (2 Cor. 11:4). The devil doesn't want the glorification of our sovereign Redeemer or the manifestation of the Holy Spirit, so he will perhaps lead us to settle for something which is staid, merely sentimental or sheer entertainment.

Satan will divert us from any strong emphasis on the gospel or on sovereign grace; from the blood of Jesus or the majesty of God. He will also try to lead us away from any working of the unbound Spirit in the Church. All his intelligence and powers of deception will be directed either towards a dilution of the gospel or a quenching of the Spirit.

Thirdly, Satan is out to demoralise: 'Now is come salvation, and strength, and the kingdom of our God, and the power of Christ: for the accuser of our brethren is cast down, which accused them before our God day and night' (Rev. 12:10).

How does Satan accuse? Sometimes he tells us that we are not saved. Or if he can't succeed with that, he tries to convince us that God has finished with us and that we are irreparably out of his will. Nothing is more demoralising to a Christian than this. But let me give you a rule of thumb here: all oppression is of the devil. Dr Martyn Lloyd-Jones used to say to me, 'God *never* oppresses us.'

Another method of accusing and demoralising us is to tell us that we are not fit to worship God as we are. The devil reminds us of some weakness or failing in our life – as a Christian or a student or a parent – and he says,

'You must get that right before you can worship God. You let others do the worshipping today. You're not in a fit state to do anything.' He tries to get in during the week, and if he fails there he tries on Sunday morning. If we lose our temper, or give in to some other weakness, he says to us: 'You're not fit.' But God never says that.

A third way Satan tries to demoralise us is by creating disturbances in worship. It may be a baby crying, a drunk shouting out or any untimely disturbances that get us to say, 'Oh, what's the use?' It is by demoralising the saints that Satan succeeds in getting revival to tarry.

When Satan succeeds he can say, 'I'm not going to have any problems there today!' And we will not even realise that the Spirit has gone. Remember that Samson, 'wist not that the Lord was departed from him' (Judges 16:20). We will only find out later, when we try to do something and realise we are doing it in our own strength. Remember, though, that we cannot lose our salvation, for Paul says, 'Grieve not the Holy Spirit of God, whereby ye are *sealed* unto the day of redemption' (Eph. 4:30).

So what are we to do in the face of Satan's strategies? The answer is that we must refuse to give place to him. We must realise that Satan's strategy is aimed to produce one thing – a grieved Holy Spirit. That is all he wants. And if he achieves that, then he has won.

But look at Revelation 12:11: 'And they overcame him by the blood of the Lamb, and by the word of their testimony; and they loved not their lives unto the death.'

The blood of Jesus tells me that I can always worship God. Yes, I am unworthy. Yes, I have sinned. Yes, I am not all that I ought to be. But that is why Jesus died. In the words of John Newton:

> Be thou my shield and hiding-place,
> That sheltered near thy side,
> I may my fierce accuser face,
> And tell him thou hast died.

The blood of Jesus is a free invitation to worship God now. Whoever we are and whatever our state, we can always resort to the blood, and that brings us up to the level of the most worthy 'saint'.

Just as I am, without one plea,
But that thy blood was shed for me,
And that thou bidst me come to thee,
O, Lamb of God, I come.

God wants us to believe this, but Satan wants us to doubt it because when we are convinced that the blood of Jesus was shed for us, we are on our way, and Satan falls.

The saints must affirm unashamedly that God has accepted them. They overcome the devil not only through the blood of Jesus, but by 'the word of their testimony'. It is one thing to have the blood of Jesus offered to us; it is another to act upon it, confident that nothing can stop us. When we affirm by the word of our testimony all that the blood of Jesus was meant to do, then Satan vanishes as quickly as darkness dispelled by light.

It is by the word of our testimony that we prove we are indeed resisting the devil. In terms of worship, we are to enter into the praying and the preaching and the singing with all our hearts, and shut everything else out. We are to let ourselves get caught up in the joy of all that is happening.

The final aspect of the saint's strategy is selfless concern: 'and they loved not their lives unto death'. When we are caught up into spiritual worship, self-concern diminishes to nothing. Self-love is swallowed up by a love for God's glory.

Something else which will also vanish is self-consciousness — what others may think of us. There is a warning here: Satan will conquer us to the extent that we allow self-concern to preoccupy our thoughts. But there is also a promise: the extent to which we become enamoured with the grace and mercy and blood of Christ, is the extent to which we will find ourselves living in the realm out of which martyrs are born.

Joseph Ton said, 'The most dangerous person in the world is the man who is not afraid to die.'

'They loved not their lives unto the death.' May our worship leave us in a state of selfless love for Jesus. Then we will be able to face any obstacle: the office, the friend who betrayed us, our besetting sin, that overwhelming worry, that dreadful fear and every attack of Satan. Why? Because God accepts us, and that is what matters: 'If God be for us, who can be against us?' (Rom. 8:31).

CHAPTER 16

... WITH GIVING

'Bring ye all the tithes into the storehouse ... and prove me now herewith, saith the Lord of hosts, if I will not open you the windows of heaven, and pour you out a blessing, that there shall not be room enough to receive it.' (Malachi 3:10)

I believe that not only is giving a part of worship, but that it may constitute a much greater part than many of us have thought. I say this for three reasons. I can give the first by reminding you of the definition of worship which I gave in Chapter 1: worship is the response to, and/or preparation for, the preached word. How we respond to the preached word will show how much we truly worship. And how we respond to, and prepare for, God's call to give according to the undoubted biblical pattern will largely reflect the quality of our worship.

The second reason I have for saying that giving is an integral part of worship is that worship must be a matter of the heart. And I am absolutely convinced that having a stingy heart – a mean spirit – inhibits our worship. Imagine that you have put a strong rubber band round your fingers, and now you are trying to open them. You just won't be able to, until the band is cut or released in some way. Well, I believe that many people are in bondage, and would like to break out, but haven't succeeded because they have not made the commitment to tithe.

My third reason is that in the Old Testament tithing consistently reflected the response of gratitude which the Patriarchs felt towards God. And these towering figures – Abraham, Isaac, Jacob – were raised up by God four hundred years before the Law came. This is a vital point. It is not true that to decide to tithe is to go back to a life lived under law: it is to return to the example set by Abraham. And the heart of Paul's teaching is that we take our cue on how we become Christians and how we live the Christian life from Abraham.

Jesus said, 'Your father Abraham rejoiced to see my day: and he saw it, and was glad' (John 8:56). And Paul said, 'They which are of faith, the same are the children of Abraham' (Gal. 3:7). The Law came in later, but it could not ignore the promise God made to Abraham.

Abraham's story is thrilling. His nephew, Lot, had been caught and captured in the crossfire of a war which was going on between several kings. God enabled Abraham not only to rescue Lot, but to retrieve Lot's possessions and gain much other spoil as well. At which point Melchizedek, king of Salem, who is called in Genesis 14:18: 'the priest of the most high God', came to Abraham and blessed him. And Genesis 14:20 says, Abraham 'gave him tithes of all'. Now one might think that Abraham could have given all the spoils to Melchizedek, because, after all, Abraham had not been expecting to gain anything when he rescued Lot. But he gave one tenth. Why the tithe? The answer is that the tithe is the consistent pattern of the Spirit for all times. When God made the decision in eternity to send his Son into the world, he knew that the gospel would have to be supported. Tithing was not an afterthought in God's scheme of things.

Abraham was not the only one who gave the tithe. Jacob crowned one of the peak moments of his life with the words, 'And of all that thou shalt give me I will surely give the tenth unto thee' (Gen. 28:22). It is a beautiful story. God had come to Jacob at a time when he felt very unworthy, having stolen the birthright from his brother Esau, and run away from home. At night he fell asleep on the bare ground, with stones for his pillow, and he had a dream – the famous vision of Jacob's Ladder. In Jacob's dream God said to him, 'Thy seed shall be as the dust of the earth, and thou shalt spread abroad to the west, and to the east, and to the north, and to the south: and in thee and in thy seed shall all the families of the earth be blessed' (Gen. 28:14).

Jacob was so overcome that God should talk to him like this that 'he called the name of that place Beth-el' (v.19). 'And Jacob vowed a vow saying, If God will be with me, and will keep me in this way that I go...then shall the Lord be my God...and of all that thou shalt give me I will surely give the tenth unto thee' (vv.20–22).

Tithing has thus always been a part of true worship, that is, worship that is of the heart and precipitated by the Spirit of God. Both Abraham and Jacob were so overwhelmed by God's goodness that they gave back a tithe.

Thus we can see that the law of Moses merely legalised tithing. What was the spontaneous and disciplined impulse of the Patriarchs was made mandatory by the Law. Hence we read in Leviticus 27:30, 'And all the tithe of the land, whether of the seed of the land, or of the fruit of the tree, is the Lord's: it is holy unto the Lord.' The tithe was the Lord's by right and those who refused to tithe were therefore punished, for, as Malachi says, 'Will a man rob God?' (Mal. 3:8). According to Malachi, ten per cent is the Lord's already, whether it is given or not. The gospel era did not introduce any new standard of righteousness. The righteousness that God requires has always been the same. But now God does not, as it were, put a pistol to our heads; instead he puts us on our honour and asks us to give from our hearts. And have we not much more reason to give gladly and gratefully than people who lived in Moses' day, since we have known the love and grace of Jesus?

Just as sin was present in the world before the Ten Commandments were set out, so tithing was God's way before the Law came in. Just as love fulfils the Law by keeping the commandments, so, I believe, a Spirit-filled, grateful man or woman who truly wants to worship God, will always be convicted to tithe. One of the reasons why people are so quick to argue against tithing is just because they are convicted, and are repressing what they know to be true. They have developed what a psychologist would call a 'reaction formation' and exhibit a great need to prove that they do not have to tithe. In the words of Shakespeare, they 'protest too much'.

It is instructive to consider Jesus' attitude to tithing. Jesus said, 'Woe unto you, scribes and Pharisees, hypocrites! for ye pay tithe of mint and anise and cummin, and have omitted the weightier matters of the law, judgment, mercy, and faith: these ought ye to have done, and not to leave the other undone' (Matt. 23:23).

Jesus is here exposing the self-righteousness of the Pharisees. Yet he ends his condemnation of them with the words, 'and not to leave the other [tithing] undone'. Jesus approved of tithing.

Many people will only do things when they 'feel led'. They are unwilling simply to accept what the Bible says, but want a special word. I have already spoken about Psalm 50:12 in connection with prayer, but it applies equally here. God says, 'If I were hungry, I would not tell thee.' In other words, we cannot guarantee that we will be so close to God that we will always catch these 'special words'. God wants us to obey his word in the Bible. On the subject of tithing, God has already spoken. Why should some people think they are so spiritual that God is going to give them special attention or tell them something different?

Some people say they disagree with tithing because it is too little – or at least the barest minimum that ought to be given. But I have discovered something about those who say this. If such people are asked to check their records, they find that, almost invariably, they do not even come up to the tenth in their giving! God wants us to show what we think of his way by having discipline, as Abraham or Jacob had discipline. Every Christian, by definition, ought to accept tithing as a commitment. To say you are a Christian means that you have taken on the name of Christ, who told us to tithe. And a Christian is a child of Abraham who set the example. Christians owe it to God to live on ninety per cent of their income. For every hundred pounds that we earn, ten pounds belongs to God. If we make six thousand pounds a year, we will have to put six hundred pounds into the storehouse.

I know that most Christians don't tithe because they have never been taught it – which is why I am taking such care to explain the principles.

I would like to give you some advice – and I know what I am talking about. I was a Jonah on this subject, and ran away, until God swallowed me up. Just after my wife and I were married, we were under great financial pressure. I came home one day feeling very discouraged, and longing for a word from God. But God seemed to be hiding his face from me. The only verse I could get was Malachi 3:8: 'Will a man rob God?' I got this verse three days in a row, and I said, 'Lord, I want encouragement. I don't want that.'

I wasn't tithing then. We were so deeply in debt that I just kept saying, 'Lord, you know I have to pay my bills. You know the most religious thing I can do is to pay my bills.' That was the way I justified not tithing.

But things didn't get any better. Two years later we were deeper in debt. At last, one day I decided to give God his tenth. We didn't get out of debt in a month or even a year. It took two years. But it happened, and now I wouldn't not tithe for anything in the world. And I have lived that way for twenty-five years.

The practical advice I want to give out of my experience is this: take the tithe off the top before any other bill is paid. Consider that ten per cent 'hot money' and give it to God as quickly as you can. Let it lie around and you will spend it every time. You will say, 'Well, God understands we have to pay the milk bill, and the money's right there.' There will always be something to use the money up.

A lot of people tithe fairly regularly, and think that's enough. But how would your husband or wife feel if you were faithful for fifty-one weeks of the year, but were unfaithful for the other week? So how do you think God feels when we hold back and justify what we keep for ourselves by saying, 'God knows I have to pay my bills'?

Paul taught the Corinthians to be disciplined and regular in their tithing. He said, 'Upon the first day of the week let every one of you lay by him in store, as God hath prospered him' (1 Cor. 16:2). Note that we are not all asked to give the same amount. Tithing is very fair. The wealthy man must pay as much for a loaf of bread or a pound of minced beef as the poor man. But when it comes to your income, God says, 'You keep ninety per cent – I'll take ten per cent.'

The wealthy man will be taxed by the Inland Revenue at a rate of forty, fifty or sixty per cent. But God only wants ten per cent.

In 2 Corinthians 9 Paul shows, firstly, that he has taught these people the importance of giving, and, secondly that they had, as a result of this, become a great example to others. Verse 2 says, 'For I know the forwardness of your mind.' The Phillips translation is, 'I know how willing you are.' The NIV puts it, 'I know your eagerness to help.' Paul had not seen the Corinthians for a while, and he felt led of the Spirit to remind them of certain principles. So in effect he says, 'I have been bragging about you, and now that I'm coming to you again I know you won't forget that, or what I am going to tell you.' This indicates that we not only need to be taught the principles of giving, but that we all need to be reminded of them.

What are the principles which Paul lays down here?

The first is that giving will do as much for us as it does for those who receive the money. As J. B. Phillips puts it: 'Giving not only helps the one who receives.' Paul says, 'He which soweth sparingly shall reap also sparingly; and he which soweth bountifully shall reap also bountifully' (2 Cor. 9:6). And have you not found this to be true?

Paul tells us here that God is a rewarder. Many people maintain that they do not want any reward. All right – that's fine. But most of us are weak enough and human enough to need a little motivation. And God will give it to us. He wants us to know that he blesses those who tithe. His word says, 'Honour the Lord with thy substance, and with the firstfruits of all thine increase: so shall thy barns be filled with plenty, and thy presses shall burst out with new wine' (Prov. 3:9–10). Dr O. S. Hawkins comments, 'When the Church releases their tithe to God and become hilarious givers, that's when the windows of blessing in spiritual measure will be poured out.'

'Bring ye all the tithes into the storehouse,' said Malachi, 'that there may be meat in mine house' (Mal. 3:10). In Malachi's day, 'storehouse' meant the Temple, and today it means our own local church. God loves the Church – it is the apple of his eye – and the tithe should go to the Church. If you can give more than the tenth, then you are free to distribute it elsewhere, to Christian work at home and overseas, but the tithe must go to the storehouse of the Church.

Paul's second principle is that giving, in order to be a part of the worship, must come from the heart. 'Every man according as he purposeth in his heart, so let him give' (2 Cor. 9:7). This is because we are not under the law of Moses, but of Christ. God puts us on our honour, and at the end of the day we have to decide whether we believe that this is God's way for us or not. And God wants us to be generous and glad in our giving: 'for God loveth a cheerful giver' (v.7).

I come now to the last of Paul's principles: God wants not only our tithe, but also our trust. This is how Paul puts it in 2 Corinthians 9:8: 'And God is able to make all grace abound towards you; that ye, always having all sufficiency in all things, may abound to every good work.' I like the way the NIV translates the phrase 'all grace abound'. It says, 'He will make you rich in every way.'

When we worship God and trust him, when we give him money which we could have kept for ourselves and used well, over the months and the years we will watch a mathematical impossibility take place. We will see the ninety per cent of our money go as far as a hundred per cent would have gone, and sometimes even further. I don't understand it, but this is what happens.

So make a commitment today that you are going to live like this for the rest of your life. You will then find that you are not burdened and tied up by worries and fears about money. Frequently someone will come up to me and say, 'Thank you for teaching me how to tithe.' These people have discovered for themselves that when we trust and obey God, then he sets our spirits free, because he loves to give back to us. And when our spirits are free, then we can worship him from an overflowing and grateful heart.

CHAPTER 17

... WITH FASTING

*'But thou, when thou fastest . . . fast . . . unto thy Father
which is in secret . . .' (Matthew 6:17–18)*

Like tithing, many of us may not find the subject of fasting pleasant, because it comes down to the disciplined
impulse of the Spirit, but its rewards may well exceed our
greatest expectations. In fact, the more I have thought
about this subject, the more I have realised that if enough
people in a church took fasting seriously, its impact on
the worship could be quite dramatic.

Fasting is going without food to achieve a particular
end. It is a means to an end. There are non-religious
reasons for fasting: we may fast for health reasons, for
example, or people may fast as a protest to get the attention of the authorities and of world opinion. But I do not
want to deal with that kind of public demonstration, and
neither do I necessarily recommend it.

The Bible gives numerous accounts of fasting for
spiritual reasons. It is often a sign of grief and mourning
– even of desperation. We read in Esther chapter 4:
'When Mordecai perceived all that was done, Mordecai
rent his clothes, and put on sackcloth with ashes, and
went out in to the midst of the city, and cried with a loud
and bitter cry; and came even before the king's gate: for
none might enter into the king's gate clothed with

sackcloth. And in every province, whithersoever the king's commandment and his decree came, there was great mourning among the Jews, and fasting, and weeping, and wailing; and many lay in sackcloth and ashes' (vv.1–3).

Fasting is not something one does flippantly, with joy or gladness. Yet the New Testament assumption is that the disciples of Jesus should, and in fact do, fast. Jesus said, 'Moreover when ye fast, be not, as the hypocrites, of a sad countenance' (Matt. 6:16). Mark 2:19–20 says: 'And Jesus said unto them, Can the children of the bridechamber fast, while the bridegroom is with them? As long as they have the bridegroom with them, they cannot fast. But the days will come, when the bridegroom shall be taken away from them, and then shall they fast in those days.'

The question of all of us is, therefore: is fasting something we should do in our twentieth-century churches, and if so, when should we fast?

According to the Bible, the people who fast fall into three categories. Firstly, a nation. We read in Isaiah 58:2–3: 'Yet they seek me daily, and delight to know my ways, as a nation that did righteousness, and forsook not the ordinance of their God ... Wherefore have we fasted, say they ...' And in the book of Nehemiah we see that the people of Israel felt the need to fast: 'Now in the twenty and fourth day of this month the children of Israel were assembled with fasting, and with sackclothes, and earth upon them.'

So it is possible for a whole nation to fast. In this country it is an unusual occurrence, but it has happened, although I am sorry to say that it was over forty years ago. The last time this nation had a day of prayer and fasting was in the middle of World War Two.

But the Church may also fast. We read in Acts 13:2–3 that, 'As they [the Church] ministered to the Lord, and fasted, the Holy Ghost said, Separate me Barnabas and

Saul for the work whereunto I have called them. And when they had fasted and prayed, and laid their hands on them, they sent them away.' And the 'they' to whom Jesus refers in Mark 2:20 is also the Church, the Bride of Christ: 'But the days will come, when the bridegroom shall be taken away from them, and then shall they fast in those days.'

Lastly, an individual may fast. Moses fasted for forty days. Jesus fasted for forty days. And it was not unusual for David to fast. In Psalm 35:13 he says, 'But as for me, when they were sick, my clothing was sackcloth: I humbled my soul with fasting . . .' Read also Psalm 109:24: 'My knees are weak through fasting.'

The apostle Paul speaks of himself and his fellow-workers in these words: 'In all things approving ourselves as ministers of God . . . in stripes, in imprisonments, in tumults, in labours, in watchings, in fastings . . .' (2 Cor. 6:4–5). And again in 2 Corinthians 11:27 he says, 'In weariness and painfulness, in watchings often, in hunger and thirst, in fastings often . . .'

When we read that people like Moses or David, Paul or our Lord Jesus Christ were given to fasting, we may see an answer to the question of why there is such a dearth of spiritual greatness at the present time. And if fasting is something new to us, we must ask ourselves whether God is leading us to engage in this particular spiritual enterprise.

This brings me to a consideration of the times when we should fast, for you might be thinking, 'I'm willing to fast, but when do I do it?' I would therefore like to suggest five occasions on which fasting is justifiable.

I think the first of these would be when the burden we are under is so great that we do not really have a desire for food – for this may be a hint from God that we should fast. David experienced a time of great mourning when God smote the son born to him as a result of his adultery with Bathsheba. In 2 Samuel 12:15–16 we read, 'And the

Lord struck the child that Uriah's wife bare unto David, and it was very sick. David therefore besought God for the child; and David fasted, and went in, and lay all night upon the earth.'

The second occasion which justifies fasting is when we are about to embark on a very great task for God, or have to take an important decision. At the beginning of his ministry, after his baptism, Jesus fasted. We read in Matthew 4:2: 'And when he had fasted forty days and forty nights, he was afterward an hungered.' And we have just seen how the Church 'fasted and prayed' before they sent Barnabas and Saul away to their work. Moreover, we are told of these two themselves, 'When they had ordained them elders in every church, and had prayed with fasting, they commended to them to the Lord, on whom they believed' (Acts 14:23).

Perhaps you are conscious, as you read this, of something unusual ahead for which you need God's help. It may be, therefore, that in anticipation of what lies ahead, you should fast. Maybe you need to know God's will and don't know what to do. It is justifiable to fast because you need wisdom for something out there in the future.

A third reason is if we feel that God is hiding his face. When God does this, it may be a form of chastening: 'For whom the Lord loveth he chasteneth, and scourgeth every son whom he receiveth' (Heb. 12:6). Perhaps we are in a rut, or have known better days spiritually. Perhaps God is not as real as we have known him to be, and we are not sure whether we have grieved him or whether he has just chosen to hide his face for reasons we can't understand. When this happens, is it important to us? Is it something we really care about? If so, maybe we ought to fast. Perhaps God is hiding his face from us in order to drive us to our knees to seek him. Joel wrote: 'Therefore also now, saith the Lord, turn ye even to me with all your heart, and with fasting, and with weeping, and with mourning: and rend your heart, and not your garments, and turn unto the Lord your God: for he is gracious and merciful, slow to anger, and of great kindness, and repenteth him of the evil. Who knoweth if he will return and repent, and leave a blessing behind him . . . ?' (Joel 2:12–14).

The fourth occasion is when we have experienced delay in the answers to our prayers. In the Old Testament in particular we have accounts of situations where God did not step in as it had been hoped he would, and as a result the people fasted. In Ezra 8:22 the writer says, 'For I was ashamed to require of the king a band of soldiers and horsemen to help us against the enemy in the way: because we had spoken unto the king, saying, The hand of our God is upon all them for good that seek him; but his power and his wrath is against all them that forsake him.' So he didn't go to the king. Instead, verse 23 says, 'So we fasted and besought our God for this: and he was intreated of us.'

Daniel, in the time of the captivity, realised one day that according to Jeremiah the prophet the captivity was only to last seventy years, and we read in chapter 9:3: 'And I set my face unto the Lord God, to seek by prayer and supplications, with fasting, and sackcloth and ashes.' So there is good reason to fast when there is a delay in answer to prayer, or if you are not sure that God is going to step in.

How much do we really care that God should speak to us and answer our prayers? Missing a meal isn't a great discipline for some. But if you enjoy eating – and most of us do – then fasting is a good test of how important something is to us.

The fifth occasion which justifies fasting is when we feel the need of unusual power which we don't have. I base this assertion on the account in Matthew 17 of a case of demon possession, a case which was too big for the disciples to handle. When they asked, 'Why could not we cast him out?' (v.19), Jesus first said, 'Because of your unbelief: for verily I say unto you, if ye have faith as a grain of mustard seed, ye shall say unto this mountain, Remove hence to yonder place; and it shall remove; and nothing shall be impossible unto you' (v.20).

But he also gave them another reason: 'Howbeit this kind goeth not out but by prayer and fasting' (v.21). Fasting should not, of course, be viewed as a way of twisting God's arm. We are not putting emotional pressure on God. We can't say, 'Now I've fasted, you can see I'm serious, so please do your bit.' Fasting is a way of ensuring that we are completely dependent upon God and open to him. It seeks spiritual emptiness and cleansing, and enables us to hear God speaking. In order to achieve this, our approach to fasting is very important.

First, fasting must be secret. Jesus said in Matthew 6:16–18: 'Moreover when ye fast, be not, as the hypocrites, of a sad countenance: for they disfigure their faces, that they may appear unto men to fast. Verily I say unto you, They have their reward. But thou, when thou fastest, anoint thine head, and wash thy face; That thou appear not unto men to fast, but unto thy Father which is in secret: and thy Father, which seeth in secret, shall reward thee openly.'

There will always be a temptation to share with others the fact that we are fasting. In the time of the Pharisees, it was a sign of piety, and they would come out in public looking sad and mournful, to let everybody see that they were fasting.

When I was a teenager, about fourteen or fifteen years old, God gave me a heart after his. When I came across this verse in Matthew and read the words, 'Anoint thy head,' I wanted to get it right. So I found some olive oil, and anointed myself with it, and then I went into a closet and shut the door. I wanted to be in secret and do it right.

Maybe God smiled when he saw me – but he was with me in those days. When we are fasting we must not let the slightest hint of it leak out. Only God needs to know. And he who 'seeth in secret, shall reward thee openly'.

The second thing is that fasting must be special. I question if it ought to be done regularly. I don't see fasting as something to be done whether you really need to or not, for example, making a commitment to fast every Friday. I think if it is used that way it will lose its significance.

Thirdly, as we have seen, fasting must have a purpose. We must know what we want to achieve. It's not like taking vitamins in the general hope that they will do us good. The fourth point is that fasting must be sensible. Some people cannot fast for medical reasons. If, for example, you are a diabetic, then that ought to disqualify you. And we must never fast without drinking a lot of liquids. There are various degrees of fasting. You can cut out one meal, or two meals, or fast for a whole day or a number of days. However, anyone seeking to fast for more than two or three days should first seek advice from an experienced Christian minister or counsellor.

After a couple of days you start feeling very good. There is nothing spiritual in this. It's merely due to changes in the body chemistry: which is why it is good to fast for physical reasons. So don't think after two days, 'Ah – God has spoken to me!' In fact, don't look for any great breakthrough while you are fasting. It can come then, of course, but the results usually come weeks later.

A fifth thing is that fasting must be spontaneous: that is, voluntary and from the heart. In my opinion there could be danger in corporate fasting, for some may be acting reluctantly and under pressure. Another difficulty about corporate fasting is that those who are taking part may be tempted to feel very self-righteous. They may judge those who are not, and ask why they are not joining in. This sort of behaviour lets the devil in.

The situation needs to be very urgent before a church calls for a day of prayer and fasting, and if it does happen, nobody must know who is taking part. There might be a case for a group to get together discreetly and covenant to fast, but the members of the group would have to be very careful not to become self-righteous or judgmental.

The next thing I need to say is that fasting must be sacrificial. Isaiah 58 describes people who fasted, but who loved it. The prophet said, 'Behold, in the day of your fast ye find pleasure' (Is. 58:3b). In the summer of 1984 I was in the Florida Keys. I had a particular burden about decision-making, and I fasted for three days. I could have gone out and bonefished while I was fasting. But I didn't, because I knew that would have been a mockery. I couldn't fast and go out fishing. No – fasting is a time of sacrifice, and if there is not some element of sacrifice I question whether the fasting will be honoured by the Holy Spirit.

Finally, we must be quite clear about our motives. And we must not have mixed motives. If you want to fast for physical reasons, then say so. But don't say, 'I need to lose a little weight, and get help about this problem. So I think I'll kill two birds with the one stone and fast.'

There is one final point. Could it be that some of us need to practise a different form of fasting? Perhaps we need to abstain from our favourite television programme, for example, or fast from judging others? This is what the people of Israel were called to do in Isaiah 58. The people were enjoying fasting, but Isaiah said, 'Is not this [rather] the fast that I have chosen? to loose the bonds of wickedness, to undo the heavy burdens . . . take away from the midst of thee . . . the putting forth of the finger, and speaking vanity' (vv.6, 9). Fasting by itself is no magic answer to our problems. It is only effective when it symbolises a deep longing for spiritual reality, and it demands a life of holiness and obedience to God. 'Then,' says God in Isaiah 58:8, 'shall thy light break forth as the morning, and thine health shall spring forth speedily.'

CHAPTER 18

... WITH SINGING

'Sing unto the Lord with thanksgiving . . .' (Psalm 147:7)

In our attempt to discover the quality and components of true worship, our touchstone has been Paul's words in Philippians 3:3: 'For we are the circumcision, who worship by the Spirit of God.' We now come to ask, 'What about singing? Can it be by the Spirit?' Of course, for most people, worship and singing are synonymous, but we have been seeing that there is much more to worship than singing. Moreover, we have been trying to look at first principles and in our understanding of worship we are seeking to include only what springs from the impulse of the Spirit. What, then, is the place of singing?

To find out, let's look at the teaching of the Bible.

The first reference to singing in the Bible comes in Exodus 15:1. Israel had just witnessed the wrath of God poured out upon the firstborn of Egypt. But God had said, 'When I see the blood, I will pass over you' (Exod. 12:13). So those who had honoured Moses' word and had sprinkled blood on door posts and lintel were spared the plague. Then had come the even greater miracle of the crossing of the Red Sea on dry land – probably the most spectacular single miracle in the Old Testament. And now in chapter 15 we find: singing.

From this we can see five things. First, that it is a

response of gratitude to God. Notice how it is put: 'Then sang Moses and the children of Israel this song unto the Lord, and spake, saying, I will sing unto the Lord . . .' (v.1). Never had the people of God been so grateful. They recalled the bitter days under Pharaoh. Days they had thought would last for ever. But now they were free. Pharaoh could never bother them again; when his army had started after them, the waters had poured back and all had been drowned. They were wonderfully saved from their enemies. No wonder they sang in gratitude to God.

What about us? The people of Israel had something to sing about – but so, surely, does every Christian. Once we were in bondage to sin and on the road to hell. We lived in fear, guilt and shame. But now we are delivered, and the past will never be held against us. 'As far as the east is from the west, so far hath he removed our transgressions from us' (Ps. 103:12). Surely every Christian church ought to be a singing church.

The second thing about the singing in Exodus 15 is that the people were rejoicing as they sang: 'Then sang Moses and the Children of Israel this song unto the Lord, and spake, saying, I will sing unto the Lord, for he hath triumphed gloriously – the horse and his rider hath he thrown into the sea. The Lord is my strength and my song . . .' One thing I have learned from all the references I have found to singing in the Bible is that it is synonymous with rejoicing. Look at the Song of Solomon 2:11–12: 'For, lo, the winter is past, the rain is over and gone; the flowers appear on the earth; the time of the singing of birds is come, and the voice of the turtle is heard in our land.' Or Isaiah 54:1, 4a: 'Sing, O barren, thou that didst not bear; break forth into singing, and cry aloud, thou that didst not travail with child: for more are the children of the desolate than the children of the married wife, saith the Lord . . . Fear not; for thou shalt not be ashamed.' And James says, 'Is any among you afflicted?

Let him pray. Is any merry? Let him sing psalms' (5:13). When we sing in church we should sound and look as though we are rejoicing. Our singing is then a testimony to those who are lost. One of the reasons the charismatic movement is growing is that there is such lively and happy singing. When lost people come into these services they say, 'I'm not happy – but these people are.' Would that all services caused an unsaved person to say, 'I want what these people have.'

The third thing about the singing of the Children of Israel with Moses is that it was an immediate response to God's extraordinary deliverance. I fear that much of what we sing about is related to events in the distant past. Perhaps when we sing we are remembering the days of our conversion twenty or thirty years ago. But it is hard to get excited about something that happened so long in the past. What has God been doing in our life lately? What happened last week? Or yesterday? Or this morning? If we can think of nothing, then that is perhaps why our singing has turned into another external form. The singing revealed an attitude of reverence, awe and wonder. The people focused on the greatness of God: 'Who is like unto thee, O Lord, among the gods? who is like thee, glorious in holiness, fearful in praises, doing wonders?' (v.11). There was simultaneous joy and fear: 'The people shall hear, and be afraid: sorrow shall take hold on the inhabitants of Palestina' (v.14). Reverence that is by the Holy Spirit is not the melancholy, staid attitude which some people call reverence and worship. It affirms the justice and holiness of God and rises spontaneously within us after we have seen God at work. The people of Israel had just seen what God had done to Pharaoh's army – and it had nearly scared them to death. They realised that God is no respecter of persons, and what he had done to the Egyptians he could do to them.

Notice that the Israelites sang their song *unto the Lord* (Exod. 15:1). When we sing, we are not singing to each other. We are responding to the Lord by singing to him. And if we were to become keenly aware that God is watching us and listening to us, would it not cause us to take notice and to sing with more reverence, attention and gratitude, and with less worry about what other people are thinking?

Finally, the singing was a responsibility laid upon the people by Moses. It was the least the people could do. And so it should be with us. As I was preparing this chapter, I found a verse in the Bible which I had never noticed before. It reads: 'And Jehoiada appointed the offices of the house of the Lord by the hand of the priests the Levites, whom David had distributed in the house of the Lord' – and here is the interesting bit – 'to offer the burnt offerings of the Lord, as it is written in the Law of Moses, with rejoicing and with singing, as it was ordained by David' (2 Chron. 23:18). Do you see what it is saying here? Singing was not anything new in David's day, but it was so important to David that he got the credit for ordaining it. But David did more than just ordain singing. In those days they did not have a rich hymnody to draw upon. They often had to compose something right on the spot. How many times does David say, 'I will sing a new song unto the Lord'? The song of Exodus 15 was a new song. David sang one psalm after another, and they were always new psalms. But many of us just want the same old thing. And we try to cover our steps by saying, 'I'm just old-fashioned.' But when there is joy, and when the Spirit is coming down, he is always moving us forward. Isaac Watts grew up complaining about the 'boring' psalms he had to sing – so his father challenged him to produce something better. And he gave us such hymns as, *When I survey the wondrous cross* and *Alas and did my Saviour bleed?* Charles Wesley could have said, 'Well, we've got Isaac Watts and the psalms.' Yet God led him to write six thousand hymns. And John Newton was criticised because he wrote a new hymn every week and

155

taught it to his congregation each Sunday night. We would perhaps not wish to sing *all* that was composed by Watts or Newton or Wesley – just as not *all* that is being composed nowadays is good. But we should be open to the new.

Perhaps you have wondered why it says at the beginning of so many psalms, 'To the Chief Musician'? Or, as the NIV puts it, 'To the Director of Music'? Well, this is because the one hundred and fifty psalms in the Bible were originally sung to prescribed music. For example, there was a tune called *Do not destroy,* which was used for Psalms 57, 58, 59 and 75. (When we get to heaven we will find out what it sounded like!)

This shows that in those days musicians and singers employed the practice common today of setting new words to an old tune.

The little word *Selah* in the middle of many psalms was originally a direction for the conductor who was leading the instruments, and indicated an interlude where the orchestra would play a little bit before the singing started again.

There is evidence both in Scripture and in the Rabbinic sources that the art of singing, particularly singing for the Temple, was diligently cultivated. 1 Chronicles 25:6–9 says, 'All these were under the hands of their father for song in the house of the Lord, with cymbals, psalteries, and harps, for the service of the house of God, according to the king's order to Asaph, Jeduthun, and Heman. So the number of them, with their brethren that were instructed in the songs of the Lord, even all that were cunning, was two hundred fourscore and eight. And they cast lots, ward against ward, as well the small as the great, the teacher as the scholar. Now the first lot came forth for Asaph . . .' (And Asaph is often mentioned in the psalms as a chief musician.) So not only was music and singing brought in, but it was not second class singing. It was to be done skilfully and professionally. There is even a hint in the Talmud (the Rabbinic commentary upon Scripture) that a failure to sing correctly annulled the value of the sacrifice. But in any case, this reference shows how seriously singing was taken. If someone was going to sing, they wanted him to sing well. In fact, the training of Levitical singers involved at least five years of intensive preparation.

This indicates that we should take care to sing to the best of our ability. Slovenly, careless and half-hearted singing does nothing to glorify God. It also shows the important role of a church choir, where those who are gifted in singing can lead the congregation out in worship. To sing in the choir is a responsibility and a calling from God.

A very dear friend of mine pulled out of a larger denomination to start his own reformed church. Overreacting, he made the architect draw up plans which would make it impossible to have a choir in the new church. But after two or three years the singing was so dead and dismal that they found a place for a choir after all.

And working on this chapter I saw something else which I hadn't seen before. In Ephesians 5:19 Paul counsels the people to speak to each other, 'In psalms and hymns and spiritual songs, singing and making melody in your heart to the Lord.' Then in verse 18, Paul says, 'And be not drunk with wine, wherein is excess, but be filled with the Spirit.'

Now in the Greek language they had no punctuation marks. The text just kept on going, which means that these verses ran together. So from that you could ask the question, 'Is "making melody in your heart" the *effect* of being filled with the Spirit, or the *means* of being filled with the Spirit?' Is Paul here asking the people first to be filled with the Spirit, and then to speak to themselves 'in psalms . . . making melody in your heart to the Lord'? Let anyone who is praying to be filled with the Spirit put these two verses together, and take Paul seriously. We may want praise to flow from our lives spontaneously, but Isaiah talks of putting on 'the garment of praise' (61:3). And the psalmist speaks of offering 'sacrifices of joy' (Ps. 27:6). Sometimes we just don't feel like singing. But we have so much to be thankful for that we must just do it. There is even a case for singing in private. Paul says, 'making melody in your heart'. God doesn't expect us all to have great voices. He doesn't care how well we can carry a tune – and some of us couldn't carry a tune in a bucket! But God sees the heart and the melody is there.

Paul says, 'I will sing with the Spirit, and I will sing with the understanding also' (1 Cor. 14:15). May God grant us to sing with the Spirit, and to sing with the understanding. And above all, to sing to him and to no one else. If every congregation did that, the worship in our churches would take off as it never has before. It would be a testimony to the lost – and God would be glorified.

CHAPTER 19

... WITH MUSIC

'Praise him with the sound of the trumpet: praise him with the psaltery and harp. Praise him with the timbrel and dance: praise him with stringed instruments and organs. Praise him upon the loud cymbals: praise him upon the high sounding cymbals ... Praise ye the Lord.' (Psalm 150:3–6)

I have had great joy in working on the material in this chapter, not merely because of the many things I have learned, but because music means so much to me. I have always understood how Martin Luther could say that next to theology, he loved music. My mother made me start taking piano lessons when I was eight years old. I used to protest then at having to practise – but the day came when I was giving concerts. And I developed a love for classical music, particularly the Russian composers. I also learned to play the oboe, and through that discovered Handel. In fact, I could have made playing the oboe my career. Music does something for me at the natural level. Like Saul, who was 'refreshed' when David played the harp, I know the feeling of being low and having music lift my spirit.

And if there is one thing which I love more than a symphony orchestra, it is a pipe organ. When I first started preaching I used to dream that some day God would let me be pastor of a church with a pipe organ. Well, I never dreamed that the church would be in London, but I gather that the organ at Westminster Chapel is one of the three or four finest instruments in London. If music can do something for the spirit at the natural level, how much more ought talented, Spirit-led Spirit-controlled music lead our spirits out to worship God?

If I have learned anything in the preparation of this chapter, it is that God loves music. Music is of God. After all – he is the one who thought of it. Music appears throughout the Bible, but the first reference to it goes back to Genesis 4:21 where we are told that a man by the name of Jubal was 'the father of all such as handle the harp and organ'.

The last references to music come in the book of Revelation, where harps are frequently mentioned. According to Revelation, in heaven there will be both singing and instrumental music. This fact should be sufficient to refute any suggestion that the use of musical instruments in church is not biblical.

My father used to tell a story about a Bible study that took place one evening in someone's living room in Kentucky. Suddenly two elderly, saintly women looked at each other and one said, 'Do you hear that?'

The other replied, 'Yes, isn't it beautiful?' No one else in the room heard anything, but tears filled these two ladies' eyes, for they were hearing music from heaven. We don't know what that will be like, but it will be a sound which will fill us with joy. I like to think that it could be like the sound of a waterfall, or the noise of waves hitting the shore, for Jesus' voice is described as 'the sound of many waters' (Rev. 1:15).

In the time of Moses, we have the use of trumpets to call the children of Israel together and as a marching signal for the different sections of their camps. Numbers 10:1–2 says, 'And the Lord spake unto Moses, saying, Make thee two trumpets of silver; of a whole piece shalt thou make them: that thou mayest use them for the calling of the assembly, and for the journeying of the camps.' Trumpets were used to send signals. Verses 5–7 continue, 'When ye blow an alarm, then the camps that lie on the east parts shall go forward. When ye blow an alarm the second time, then the camps that lie on the south side shall take their journey . . . But when the congregation is to be gathered together, ye shall blow, but ye shall not sound an alarm.'

The concept of music as art was alien to the ancient world. Nowadays some of us go to the Royal Albert Hall simply to listen to the music – but in those days it was an organic part of life from birth to death. Music was essential. In ancient times people thought of music the way we think of flowers. You don't have to have flowers near you all the time, but you can't imagine a world without them. Music was for social merrymaking, for worship, and in war to terrorise the enemy. Judges 7:18–21 says, 'When I blow with a trumpet, I and all that are with me, then blow ye the trumpets also on every side of the camp, and say, The sword of the Lord and of Gideon . . . and they blew the trumpets . . . And they stood every man in his place round about the camp: and all the host ran, and cried, and fled.' So it was not a matter of art and pleasant listening.

Before the establishment of David's kingdom women played the major part in the performance of music. There was Miriam, with her tambourine, and Deborah, the daughter of Jepthah. In 1 Samuel 18:6–7 we read of the incident which so infuriated Saul: 'And it came to pass as they came, when David was returned from the slaughter of the Philistine, that the women came out of all cities of Israel, singing and dancing to meet king Saul, with tabrets, with joy, and with instruments of musick.'

Up to this time there were no professional musicians as we think of them today. But they began to make an appearance in David's time, and from then on we hear more about men taking the lead in music.

David, the only man in the Bible whom God called 'a man after mine own heart' (Acts 13:22), loved music. He prescribed it. He wrote it and he played it. As we saw in the last chapter, singing was ordained by David (2 Chron. 23:18). David polished and refined music and made it an integral part of worship. And the professional musician was a functionary of high rank.

An interesting question is: where did the Levites who were appointed to be musicians in the time of David get their training? It is thought that they received their instruction from professional musicians from Egypt or Assyria who were invited to Jerusalem in order to train the Israelite musicians and singers. And we do a similar thing today. When we send our children to learn music from professional teachers, we don't know if the teacher is a Christian. We just want the best teaching.

In Old Testament times there were four types of instruments (there are five today). The first category was the ideophone (which we would call percussion), where the instrument's own material produced the tone. In this group were bells, castanets, cymbals and chimes. In the second category were the aerophones, or wind instruments – the bugle, rams horn and horn, trumpet, flute, oboe and clarinet, the pipe, bagpipe and sackbut. In the third group were the membraphones, or instruments for vibration, such as the tambourine, timbrel and drum. (Today we would class the ideophones and membraphones together, as the percussion.) Finally there were the cordophones – the stringed instruments: harp, lute, psaltery, lyre, dulcimer, viol. (And today we have electronic music to add to this list.) It is also interesting to note that the harp – David's instrument – was considered the noblest of all. It was the instrument of the aristocracy, and was often made of precious woods and metals.

In 1 Chronicles 15, we find a description of the occasion when David brought the Ark to Jerusalem. David wanted to get it right this time. He had tried once before and things had gone wrong. Chapter 13 tells how on that first time, a man named Uzzah had put out his hand to steady the ark and had been struck dead. And for three months the ark had been left where it was.

On that first occasion, and now on this second occasion, it was assumed that there would be music. Chapter 15:16 says, 'And David spake to the chief of the Levites to appoint their brethren to be the singers with instruments of musick, psalteries and harps and cymbals, sounding, by lifting up the voice with joy.' It never crossed their minds to celebrate such an important event without music.

We see from 1 Chronicles 15 that music is an aid to worship. Verse 28 says, 'Thus all Israel brought up the ark of the covenant of the Lord with shouting, and with sound of the cornet, and with trumpets, and with cymbals, making a noise with psalteries and harps.' The instruments led the way so that the singers could find their tune. Psalm 33:1–3 says, 'Rejoice in the Lord, O ye righteous: for praise is comely for the upright. Praise the Lord with harp: sing unto him with the psaltery and an instrument of ten strings. Sing unto him a new song; play skilfully with a loud noise.' The music enabled the singers to find their place, and it was played skilfully and absolutely correctly.

I have already mentioned the role of a choir in worship. Music can even make or break the atmosphere in a service. I never will forget preaching some years ago in a church which had an organist whose style mirrored a recalcitrant spirit. It was very difficult to sing to his playing. There would be long pauses between some verses, and no pause at all between others and you didn't know which he would do next. It was obviously a way of making the congregation follow him, and of drawing attention to himself, and it was a very sad situation.

Someone responsible for leading the singing and music in church needs natural skill, spiritual discernment and a desire for the glory of God, not for the praise of men. And this is what David was seeking when he 'spake to the chief of the Levites to appoint their brethren to be the singers with instruments of musick, psalteries and harps and cymbals, sounding, by lifting up the voice with joy' (1 Chron. 15:16).

This brings me to the aim of music. 1 Chronicles 16:4 says, 'And he appointed certain of the Levites to minister before the ark of the Lord, and to record, and to thank and praise the Lord God of Israel.' Verses 5b and 6 go on: 'But Asaph made a sound with cymbals; Benaiah also and Jahaziel the priests with trumpets continually [NIV: 'regularly'] before the ark of the covenant of God'. And 1 Chronicles 9:33 says, 'And these are the singers, chief of the fathers of the Levites, who remaining in the chambers were free: for they were employed in that work *day and night*.' The people considered that *God* wanted to hear music even when Israel slept, for the aim of music was to praise God.

These verses help us to understand other references, such as Psalm 134:1: 'Behold, bless ye the Lord, all ye servants of the Lord, which by night stand in the house of the Lord.' Or Psalm 150: 'Praise ye the Lord. Praise God in his sanctuary ... Praise him with the sound of the trumpet: praise him with the psaltery and harp. Praise him with the timbrel and dance: praise him with stringed instruments and organs ...'

The aim of music was to bring glory to God by expressing praise and gratitude. So in Psalm 92 we read: 'It is a good thing to give thanks unto the Lord, and to sing praises unto thy name, O most High. To shew forth thy lovingkindness in the morning, and thy faithfulness every night, upon an instrument of ten strings, and upon the psaltery; upon the harp with a solemn sound' (vv.1–3).

From the time of Solomon onwards music became an accessory to the sacrificial rituals: but only an accessory. Important as the musician was, his music was not seen as an end in itself. An ominous trend in some places today is to make music almost the centre of worship. But this should not be. Music is only one part of a service of worship. You cannot worship God without his word; 'It pleased God by the foolishness of preaching to save them that believe' (1 Cor. 1:21).

But if you go to heaven, I hope you like music! God likes it so much that he has even chosen the trumpet as his way of announcing the Second Coming. 1 Corinthians 15:51 says, 'Behold, I shew you a mystery; we shall not all sleep, but we shall all be changed, in a moment, in the twinkling of an eye, at the last trump: for the trumpet shall sound, and the dead shall be raised incorruptible, and we shall be changed.' As Paul says in 1 Thessalonians 4:16, 'For the Lord himself shall descend from heaven with a shout, with the voice of the archangel, and with the trump of God.'

There *is* coming a day when God is going to sound a trumpet such as this generation or any other generation in the history of the world has never heard, for it will raise the dead. And then singing and music will go on for ever and ever in heaven. But until that day comes, thank God for good music – for Spirit-led music – which aids our worship while having as its only aim the glory of God.

CHAPTER 20

. . . WITH THE WHOLE PERSONALITY

'I beseech you therefore, brethren, by the mercies of God, that ye present your bodies a living sacrifice . . . and be not conformed to this world: but be ye transformed by the renewing of your mind, that ye may prove what is that good, and acceptable, and perfect, will of God.' (Romans 12:1–2)

When we speak of the impulse of the Spirit we are in some sense talking about feelings. I admit this is dangerous, because feelings can lead people to do strange things. This impulse may take the form of an insight that is based upon accumulated knowledge. It may be a suspicion that is based upon knowledge experienced. But the impulse of the Spirit, when obeyed, always leads to a feeling of immense peace.

One of the most helpful verses in this connection is Romans 14:19. In the NIV it reads: 'Let us therefore make every effort to do what leads to peace and to mutual edification.' The proof that the impulse of the Spirit lies behind our feeling that we ought to do something is the peace that obedience brings. This verse applies not only to a situation where tensions among people need to be defused but also to our own inmost feelings. God will never lead us to do what violates our conscience. When I am really following him, I will have an inner ease that testifies to the fact that I have been true to myself. 'To thy own self be true,' said Shakespeare. Romans 14:19 agrees! When a lack of inner peace – a heaviness or feeling of oppression – results from obeying any impulse, I know that impulse was not of God.

The reason why following the impulse of the Spirit is potentially dangerous is, first, because immature people may surmise the Spirit's impulse and be utterly, ridiculously and sadly wrong. An example of this is a horror story from near Chattanooga, Tennessee. Many years ago a sincere Christian lady felt she was led of the Holy Spirit to take literally Jesus' words, 'If thy right hand offend thee, cut it off' (Matt. 5:30). Her husband came home from work one day to find she had cut off her arm with a hatchet. It was a scandal in that area, and many people never got over the trauma.

Overly conscientious people, driven by a feeling of guilt, may seek to offset a foolish wrong action by doing something that they think is the will of God. Someone may imagine that he is feeling the impulse of the Spirit when all he is doing is making a human effort to atone for a past failure. Sometimes people think that if they go into full-time Christian work it will make what they did look better; or justify it.

Another danger is that a zealous Christian, who is anxious to see God work, may project upon God a particular idea or feeling, and then say that God is leading him or her to do it..I may call something the will of God when it's not the Spirit's impulse, but my own wish.

However, these dangers should not make us reject one of the most common assumptions in the Bible – that God made us with the capacity to grasp his leading. This inbuilt capacity that God has given us is one of the means by which God communicates to us what he is feeling. It is because of this, for example, that we experience a sense of guilt and shame. When Adam and Eve sinned, they suddenly knew they were naked and began to clothe themselves with fig leaves. This sense of guilt came from their awareness of God's attitude to sin.

It is the Holy Spirit who convicts of sin, and the only way a person will ever be converted is when the Spirit comes down. The Spirit brings home to us that we have been doing wrong. The Spirit makes us conscious of a grieved holy God.

God wants to communicate with us not just at an intellectual level. I'm touching now on a problem many of us have. It's easy to think that the only stimulation that matters is cerebral brilliance or depth. But God wants to communicate with our whole being – our emotions and senses as well as our minds.

If we suppress genuine Spirit-led feelings we put out the Spirit's fire. 1 Thessalonians 5:19 says, 'Quench not the Spirit.' The NIV says: 'Do not put out the Spirit's fire.' Why does Paul say that? He's talking about rejoicing evermore, praying without ceasing, giving thanks in everything. Then he says, 'Quench not the Spirit. Despise not prophesyings. 'It is because we all have a fear of things getting out of hand. Just as there are those who are afraid to believe in justification by faith because of the fear of lawlessness, so also there are those who want things to be done in rigid order because of the danger of fanaticism. These people are in danger of quenching the Spirit.

However, in the next verse Paul says, 'Prove all things; hold fast that which is good.' We are to use our minds. God wants us to have our heads screwed on. We are to be harmonious, whole and balanced people.

The events of the first Palm Sunday provide an illustration of the right way to worship. Here were hundreds praising the Lord Jesus as he came down from the Mount of Olives on his way to Jerusalem. The feelings of the people exploded on this Palm Sunday. They were full of expectancy and excitement. As we saw in Chapter 7, there is worship in expectancy. Donald Grey Barnhouse once said, 'While we wait we can worship.' The prelude itself is to be enjoyed. It's like the hors d'oeuvres or an appetiser at the beginning of a meal.

The people were able to express their feelings. Luke writes: 'The whole multitude of the disciples began to rejoice and praise God with a loud voice for all the mighty works that they had seen' (19:37). They had heard about Jesus. Many had seen what he had done and they began to talk together. One said, 'He changed my life.' Another said, 'You should talk to my sister. She was paralysed.' And another: 'Let me tell you what happened to me.' There were reports all over the place. On this day they thought it was all coming together. At long last what each of the people felt instinctively and individually was coalescing into one great, climactic event. They let themselves go.

Real worship takes place when we are unafraid to express what we feel. There's nothing that leads to greater pain than repressed feelings. Repression is a defence mechanism. We can't face up to what we feel, so we deny it, sometimes unconsciously, involuntarily. But we don't get rid of something by repressing it. It goes down into our subconscious and comes out later as high blood pressure or mental illness or something else.

We need to learn to express our feelings, at least to ourselves and to God. We need to admit to ourselves what we really think and feel. For example, perhaps we weren't honest about our feelings a year ago, but now we can say, 'This is the way I really felt. I see it now. I wish I had seen it then, and been true to myself at that time.'

Worship ought to bring us to the point where we can be honest right now. We never need to repress what we feel when we are around Jesus. He will never scold us for our honesty. It doesn't mean we are right, but if we are being honest, he can help us and bring us to see where we are wrong, and to face the truth.

We may envy the people's exuberance on Palm Sunday. We may say, 'I wish I could do that. I just can't get excited like this. They shouted out aloud, but that's not my nature. How could they do it?'

There's only one answer. Jesus was right there. When Jesus is there you forget everybody else and let yourself go. Possibly the highest goal in worship is simply not to be self-conscious but only conscious of Jesus. *Then* we will express our feelings!

On Palm Sunday the people's feelings were spontaneous. There was no script, no director, no order of worship. Jesus didn't say, 'Matthew, on my signal you come and read the twenty-third Psalm.' The people took over. John's account says, 'On the next day much people that were come to the feast, when they heard that Jesus was coming to Jerusalem, took branches of palm trees and went forth to meet him, and cried, Hosannah [that is, Salvation]' (12:12).

But it wasn't a coup. They weren't trying to get control. Some church leaders stamp on any spontaneous expression of feelings because they want to build their empire and are paranoid that somebody is going to try and take over. Was Jesus upset? Did he disown this demonstration? Here he was riding down the Mount of Olives on the donkey and people were spreading their clothes out in front of it and waving and shouting. Was Jesus saying, 'Don't do that. Stop it'? Of course not. Praise was due to him.

When anybody gets excited over Jesus you must let them. Someone may get carried away, and you may want to say, 'Isn't that going over the top? How embarrassing!' But it's not bothering the Lord. It's you who's got the problem. Some people criticised on that first Palm Sunday. Luke 19:39 says, 'Some of the Pharisees from the multitude said unto him, Master, rebuke thy disciples.' People like that will always be around. When revival comes there will be those stationed around taking notes to report what's going on. But Jesus will never rebuke fervent worship. Look what he said to those Pharisees: 'I tell you that, if these should hold their peace, the stones would immediately cry out' (v.40).

That was Palm Sunday — look at how much more fervent the worship was on Easter Day. In Matthew 28:9 we read: 'And as they went to tell his disciples, behold, Jesus met them, saying, All hail. And they came and *held him by the feet*, and worshipped him.'

The two Marys had just discovered the empty tomb and the angel had said, 'Go quickly, and tell his disciples that he is risen from the dead.' As they were rushing to find the disciples, Jesus met them on the way. He came to where they were, and they weren't expecting this. It was an unplanned meeting. The result was spontaneous worship: they worshipped with their bodies, on their faces on the ground. We know this because Matthew writes that they came and held him by the feet.

What about the subject of worshipping with our bodies? I believe that when it is spontaneous and not contrived, this, too, is glorifying to God. In Chapter 19 we were looking at how David brought the ark to Jerusalem. David became so excited by the atmosphere provided by the singing and the instruments that he began to dance. The Hebrew says that he made 'a swirl' around the ark. David's dancing was spontaneous, he wasn't taking directions from a choreographer. Michal's reaction shows that it was unexpected and unrehearsed: when she saw him getting carried away we are told that 'she despised him in her heart' (1 Chron. 15:29). Unspiritual people often despise those who really enjoy themselves in the Lord.

When dancing is a spontaneous response to the glory and love of God, it does bring praise to him. But it must be spontaneous and not contrived. Dancing as a planned so-called art form, I fear, draws more attention to the performance than to the adoration of God.

I preach with my body, especially when I feel free in the Spirit. We must be free to express our feelings with our bodies. In their joy and love for him the two Marys

171

held on to Jesus. There's a place for hugging in our Christian life. I'm sure people hugged each other in the New Testament. The 'holy kiss' (Rom. 16:16; 1 Cor. 16:20; 2 Cor. 13:12; 1 Thess. 5:26; 1 Pet. 5:14) was probably a hug or kiss on the cheek.

A man in our church told me that when I once told everyone to take the hand of the person they were sitting with, he looked at the person next to him and thought the man would resent it. 'But,' he said, 'I hesitated and then put my hand out to him and he took it. When it was time to break he held on a little longer and I could see that he appreciated a feeling of acceptance.' There are some people who just want to feel accepted and a touch can mean more than many words.

Jesus said to the two Marys: 'Be not afraid: go tell my brethren that they go into Galilee, and there they shall see me' (Matt. 28:10). Jesus called his followers 'brothers'. My parents hugged each other, and they hugged me. I hug my son and my daughter. When we are Christians we belong to each other: we are a family, so there is a right time to hug. But if it is not a spontaneous expression of Christian love and compassion, and if it is not mutually edifying, hugging is wrong and could be counter-productive. There are those who don't want this, and that is all right. We must be straight with each other, and respect each other's feelings.

Another mark of the Easter Day worship was that the two Marys were filled with very deep and conflicting emotions: 'they departed quickly from the sepulchre with fear and great joy' (v.8). The NIV says, 'afraid yet filled with joy'. They felt simultaneous joy and fear. This sometimes happens. In Acts 2:43 we read, 'Fear came upon every soul.' Three verses later it says, 'They, continuing daily with one accord in the temple, and breaking bread from house to house, did eat their meat with *gladness* and singleness of heart.'

Often we experience mixed feelings about something.

This can happen at a purely natural level. We may come to church, for example, feeling hopeful, or excited, and also with a natural fear and timidity. There may also be a residual unbelief which results in fear, or fear as a result of a satanic attack. This sort of fear is not from God, for Paul wrote to Timothy: 'God hath not given us the spirit of fear; but of power, and of love, and of a sound mind' (2 Tim. 1:7).

There may also be joy at the natural level. We may come to church feeling good because everything is going well. Maybe the sun is out, or we've had a pay rise, good news, or a letter from home, and we feel great. There's nothing wrong with this. Thank God for it. But it's not to be confused with spiritual joy.

God was the source of the mixed joy and fear felt by the two Marys. They didn't know what it all meant. But even though they were scared nearly to death they were filled with happiness. They knew that something wonderful was taking place. I am talking here about one of the grandest, most magnificent experiences known to man: the fear of God, the sense of awe because we can't explain it, but the tremendous joy and almost overwhelming sense of excitement because we know God is up to something.

But someone may say, 'That's all very well, but they saw Jesus with their own eyes. If I could see Jesus with my very eyes, then I too might fall at his feet and hold on to them.'

It is very easy for us to think that if only we could see Jesus we would believe and worship. Yet when we look at Jesus' resurrection appearances, we see something extraordinary. Matthew writes: 'And when they saw him, they worshipped him: *but some doubted*' (Matt. 28:17).

How could this have happened? How could anybody doubt when they are seeing? 'Seeing is believing,' it is often said, but here were some who saw but still doubted.

Yet it is not surprising when you stop to consider what we have been learning about worship. Philippians 3:3

says that we worship by the Spirit of God. It is the Spirit who reveals Jesus. And today the Spirit gives us the eyes to see as those first believers saw with their physical eyes. The more we have of the Spirit the more we will see and feel what they felt.

When Jesus went away he sent another 'Comforter' (Greek: *paraclete*, which means, literally, one who comes alongside). The Holy Spirit simply brings us right back to the way it was when Jesus was here.

Conversely, no matter how much one may see with one's eyes, if the Holy Spirit is not present one sees nothing with one's spirit, and there is no worship.

The corollary of this is that relying on sight to create a sense of worship in our services has its dangers. Without the Spirit there is the likelihood of idolatry, of worshipping a 'graven image'. C. H. Spurgeon used to say that the less we have of the Spirit, the more we will need to see physical things to inspire us. On the other hand, when we truly worship by the impulse of the Spirit, there is little need to have a lot of visual aids.

Even when Moses saw the burning bush, he was not allowed to get very close, or look for very long. The phenomenon he sighted was transcended by the word of God: 'Moses, Moses . . . draw not nigh hither: put off thy shoes from off thy feet, for the place whereon thou standest is holy ground' (Exod. 3:4–5). God may accommodate us with what is visible, as in the bread and wine at the Lord's Supper, but the end is not in seeing with our physical eyes, but 'discerning the Lord's body' by faith (1 Cor. 11:29).

The Holy Spirit gave Peter the vision on the roof in Caesarea, but again, what was seen was upstaged by what was heard: 'What God hath cleansed, that call not thou common' (Acts 10:15). Therefore, even a vision, if one be so blessed by God, is not an end in itself, but the means by which the word of God is magnified.

Last summer I came in from a day's bonefishing in the

Florida Keys. As I came away I looked back towards the sea. It was so beautiful. The sky was blue; the clouds were white and fluffy; the wind was gentle. I felt that God was saying to me, 'How do you like what I have done for you today in providing this for you?' I felt that so often we take God's creation for granted, and that God wanted to be noticed and thanked for what he has done at the natural level. Since then I have made it a point to be thankful and worship God for his creation.

Yet even creation, with all its beauty, only reveals the glory and love of God to the man who is taught by the Spirit of God. Some people see only indifference and cruelty in the created world.

The ability to see with our spirit what God is doing, and to hear with our inward ear what God is saying is God's gift to us. Some people can see more quickly than others what God is up to. It's not necessarily that the others are being rebellious, hostile or digging in their heels; they are just sincerely not sure. Does Jesus slap their wrist? Does he get on to them and say, 'Come on. Shame on you'? No. He calls attention to what he is in himself: 'All power is given unto me in heaven and in earth.' He just continues to speak. All we must do is continue to give all our attention to Jesus. C. H. Spurgeon once said: 'Look to Jesus and a dove will fly into your heart, but look to the dove and it will fly away.' And then we must obey him with our mind, and will and feelings. This quality of attention and obedience is what worshipping with the whole personality means.

And in the act of obedience doubts and fears often slip away, and we are filled with joy and trust and a true spirit of worship. A lot of people say, 'I can't start doing what God tells me to do because I'm waiting to be filled with the Spirit.' Start doing it and God will fill you! The two Marys met Jesus as they obeyed the angel. As we give our whole selves to Jesus in obedience, he meets us. And then we truly know what it means to worship in spirit and in truth.

CHAPTER 21

WORSHIP AND TRADITION

'Where the Spirit of the Lord is, there is liberty.' (2 Corinthians 3:17)

A few summers ago, when I was on holiday in Florida, I was invited to preach one Sunday morning at the Coral Ridge Presbyterian Church in Fort Lauderdale. It was a very traditional service. Everything was very formal, and we marched in with the choir down the centre aisle. I was also wearing a robe.

Later in the afternoon I flew to Bimini in the Bahamas where I planned to do some fishing on the Monday. But that Sunday evening I fulfilled an engagement to preach at the church of the Rev Sammy Ellis (who used to be known as Bonefish Sam). At that service I didn't even have a tie – I think I was wearing a sports shirt. And of the thirty or so people there, I was the only white man.

Two such opposite experiences and traditions in one day: but God was in both. God used me in that morning service – I received a number of letters about the sermon I preached. And in that little service in Bimini, while we were on our knees praying in the utmost informality, I had an insight into the text on which I was to preach (Hebrews 13:8, 'Jesus Christ the same yesterday, and to day, and for ever') which gave me a perspective on Jesus which I never got over. I also preached to that small congregation with unusual power.

It could be argued from this story that nothing is more irrelevant than tradition. The two services were quite different, and yet God was as powerfully present in the one as in the other. This is something we must always keep in mind.

The atmosphere in our churches, the way we shape our services – even our theology – are all formed by tradition. The whole of Western Christianity is shaped by the fact that our heritage goes back to the Latin Fathers (for example, St Augustine), and comes up through Thomas Aquinas and Anselm, Luther and Calvin.

If you go to the Soviet Union, where the theology derives from the Greek Fathers, you will find a vastly different tradition and different insights. There was no Reformation in Eastern Christianity, which means that Russian Orthodoxy has been the formative influence on worship in the Soviet Union today.

If we in the West were asked, 'What would you reply if God were to say to you, "Why should I let you into heaven?"' we would probably answer: 'Because Jesus died on the cross for my sins.' But if we were to ask that question among evangelicals in the Soviet Union, we would probably get the reply, 'Because Jesus was raised from the dead.' In Eastern Europe the emphasis is on the resurrection.

God has his elect scattered all over the world from all theological traditions.

This word 'tradition' means 'a handing down of opinions'. In our New Testament it is used to translate the Greek word *paradosis*, from the verb *paradidomi*, which means not so much 'hand down' as 'hand over'. The word itself is neutral: it can be good or bad. Nothing can help worship as much as tradition, and equally, nothing can hurt worship as much as tradition.

When the apostle Paul used the word it was almost always in a positive sense. In 1 Corinthians 11:2 the Greek

177

is translated in the Authorised Version as 'ordinances', but it means 'tradition': 'Now I praise you, brethren, that ye remember me in all things, and keep the ordinances, as I delivered them to you.' (That is, 'as I handed them over to you'.) And in 1 Corinthians 15:3–4 Paul writes, 'For I delivered unto you first of all that which I also received, how that Christ died for our sins according to the scriptures. And that he was buried, and that he rose again the third day according to the scriptures.' This was the most ancient tradition of the Church – and Paul was affirming it. And he affirmed it again in 2 Thessalonians 2:15, where he says, 'Therefore, brethren, stand fast, and hold the traditions which ye have been taught, whether by word, or our epistle.' In chapter 3 of the same book he says, '. . . withdraw yourselves from every brother that walketh disorderly, and not after the tradition which he received of us' (v.6).

When he used this word, Paul meant the true teachings of Jesus passed on from the apostles to the believers in the early Church.

But Jesus used the word in rather a different way, and it is this negative aspect that I want to concentrate on. Matthew 15:3 says, 'Why do ye also transgress the commandment of God by your tradition?' And verse 6 says, 'Thus have ye made the commandment of God of none effect by your tradition.' Now here Jesus was addressing the Pharisees, who had made the mistake of elevating their traditions to the level of Holy Scripture. As a result, they could no longer distinguish between what they practised, and what the word of God actually taught. Human tradition can be both blinding and binding. It blinds us from seeing things objectively, and it binds us to wrong interpretations.

Now just what was this tradition? It was the Jewish oral law, the oral tradition passed on by word of mouth until eventually someone said, 'We'd better write this up.' So we have such documents as the Mishnah and the Talmud.

The Mishnah comprises the written collection of Jewish laws which had been preserved orally since the time of Ezra (about 450 BC) and took its final form early in the third century AD. In AD 200–500 Rabbinic comments on the Mishnah were collected to form the Gemara. The Mishnah and Gemara, along with a collection of legal precepts (the Halakkah) and non-legal interpretations of these (the Haggadah) were put together to form the Talmud, dating from the sixth century AD, which all orthodox Jews now have to obey.

In this way traditions were turned into dogma which had to be believed and became the equivalent of Scripture. The same thing has happened in the West with the Roman Catholic Church. The lighting of candles, the idea of purgatory, the concept of the worship of Mary – these were all at one point innovations, but were subsequently turned into dogma. The Council of Trent of 1545 did in fact equate tradition with Scripture.

But Protestants are not free of this danger. We must be careful not to do the same, for example, with our Westminster Confession of Faith, the Thirty-nine Articles – or whatever theological confession we affirm.

'Well,' you may ask, 'what on earth does this have to do with worship?' The answer to this is – a great deal. In Matthew 15:9 Jesus quoted from Isaiah: 'But in vain do they worship me, teaching for doctrines the commandments of men' (29:13). So we see that the equating of human tradition with Scripture can lead to defective worship, what the Authorised Version calls 'vain worship'.

We all feel good in church when there are things around us with which we are familiar. But we must beware. It may be that we are merely feeling 'at home' in a certain tradition. We may like the tone of voice used in the prayer. We may be used to 'the hoil', as they say in Wales, or 'the holy tone' as we say back in the hills of Kentucky. We may like an elaborate set-up at the altar, or, if you come from Tennessee, prefer a simple wooden rail where people can go and kneel. Reformed churches have their pulpits in the centre. Some people just have a Bible in the centre, or have the pulpit off to the side because they think the Eucharist is the centre of the worship. All this is merely tradition, and the Spirit of God is not necessarily present in any of it.

What was wrong with the worship of the Pharisees? The first thing is that it was provincial. Matthew 15:1 says, 'Then came to Jesus scribes and Pharisees, which were *of Jerusalem.*' They had come all the way to Galilee, and they wanted to superimpose Jerusalem on Galilee. They were saying, in effect, 'We do it this way in Jerusalem. Why don't you do it that way up here?' If you think provincially, you can only see how things are done in a certain area.

But secondly, the worship of the Pharisees was parochial. Now to be parochial means to be narrow-minded, to feel that certain things are all-important, to the exclusion of wider issues. Verse 2 says, 'Why do thy disciples transgress the tradition of the elders? for they wash not their hands when they eat bread.' Being parochial is taking one doctrine and making everything revolve around that. If we come to a church wanting to know what the members of that church believe about baptism, or the sovereignty of God, or the baptism of the Spirit, before we make up our mind to listen, then we are being a bit parochial.

Look at what had been going on just before the Pharisees asked this question. Matthew 14:35–36 says, 'And when the men of that place had knowledge of him, they sent out into all the country round about, and brought unto him all that were diseased. And besought him that they might only touch the hem of his garment: and as many as touched were made perfectly whole.' People were being healed of diseases of all kinds, and you can imagine the talk there must have been. But the Pharisees were totally unimpressed. All they could do was ask a question about washing your hands. There is nothing in the Bible that says you must wash your hands before you eat. There's certainly nothing wrong with doing it, but it cannot be insisted upon as the infallible word of God. When the Pharisees insisted on it, their source was not the Bible but the tradition of the elders.

We find the same thing in John 9. Jesus healed a blind man and the Pharisees' reaction was, 'This man is not of God, because he keepeth not the Sabbath day' (v.16). Parochial thinking almost always leads to judgmentalism.

I never will forget the story told me by a British preacher, a friend of mine, who made a trip to America. He stopped first in West Virginia, and during the week he was there his Christian hosts frequently lamented those professing Christians who smoked or drank.

He then moved on to Grand Rapids, Michigan, which is about ninety per cent Dutch, and the centre of Reformed Calvinism. Here they have what they call the 'glorious doctrine of Christian Liberty'. He was met by their new host, who was smoking a cigar, and when they got to the house they were offered a whisky. But at the end of a Sunday in Grand Rapids they were driving down the road after church when my friend saw a Howard Johnson's restaurant and said, 'Oh, I just love their ice-cream!'

There was a silence, but their host pulled over and they all went in. Across the table my friend said, 'I know there is something wrong.'

The man replied, 'Well – this is the Sabbath, and we never buy ice-cream on the Sabbath.'

My friend said to his wife when they got home, 'You know, everybody has got to have something that they are against. I wonder what it is with us?'

The worship of the Pharisees was not only provincial and parochial – it was people worship. 'Why do thy disciples transgress the tradition of the elders?' they asked. At bottom, they worshipped people. Those who started their traditions may have been good, serious and learned men. They may have been responsible men – but they were only men. All man-made traditions have a beginning in men. Great men tend to have strong views, and they will emphasise certain things. And because they also often have strong personalities they influence their followers to accept their views. But this is only people worship.

In Matthew 15 we also see that the Pharisees' worship was legalistic – which means a preoccupation with the letter of the law at the expense of the spirit. The Pharisees were so anxious to get every tiny detail right that they ended up with over 600 laws which modified and explained the simple commandments of the Bible. The result was a distortion of God's Law. They hid behind their interpretations and ended up breaking the very Law they venerated. So Jesus said to them, 'For God commanded, saying, Honour thy father and mother: and he that curseth father or mother, let him die the death. But ye say, whosoever shall say to his father or his mother, It is a gift, by whatsoever thou mightest be profited by me; and honour not his father or his mother, he shall be free. Thus have ye made the commandment of God of none effect by your tradition' (Matt. 15:4–6).

Finally, their worship was parrot-like; it was worship by rote, by language only. They said the right things, but look at verses 7 and 8, 'Ye hypocrites, well did Esaias prophesy of you, saying, This people draweth nigh unto me with their mouth, and honoureth me with their lips; but their heart is far from me.'

Churches which follow a liturgical pattern of worship are particularly prone to this danger (though a liturgical service is not necessarily bad, as I will try to show in the next chapter). The prayers may be good and solid, the hymns brilliant; everything may be in good taste and theologically sound; the beauty of the language may give you a happy feeling: but if it is just words, it is spiritually useless.

A minister friend of mine was trying to win a prominent lawyer to his church, and finally the man agreed to come to hear him preach. So my friend worked doubly hard on his sermon, and after the service was over, thought, 'I've really done it!' And he couldn't wait to get the lawyer's reaction.

The man said, 'I've got a book in my office with every word of your sermon in it. Come round tomorrow morning and I'll show it to you.'

Well, my friend hardly slept that night. Nine o'clock the next morning found him at the office.

The lawyer handed him a dictionary and said, 'Words, preacher – just words.'

Yet that is what some people want – as if the words can somehow do the work of worship for them. They should heed the warning of the apostle Paul: 'Having a form of godliness, but denying the power thereof' (2 Tim. 3:5).

How do we know that in our worship we ourselves are not bound and blinded by tradition? The first step is by seeing that there is no such thing as one single right tradition. For what may be right for one may be wrong for someone else. We must also realise that it doesn't take any spirituality at all to uphold a tradition – however valid it may be. There are three kinds of people – tradition takers, tradition breakers and tradition makers. The first type have no discernment – they simply accept everything as it is. Someone may be converted in a charismatic church, and a week later be holding their hands up in the air. Well, it didn't take any great spirituality to do that. Equally, those of us who have never done such a thing in our whole lives are not thereby being spiritual. It is simply that we cannot conceive of ever doing it.

Tradition breakers, too, may not be spiritual. They may just want to be rebellious. As for the tradition maker, he needs to be aware that he is going to leave a legacy which may have to be broken by the next generation. It may only have been valid for one particular set of needs.

The real question we ought to ask is not, 'Is our tradition right?' but, 'How do we know that our tradition is not wrong?'

Three answers come out in Matthew 15. We know that our tradition is not wrong, firstly, if it promotes love. The Pharisees' legalistic traditions were right against love: 'For God commanded saying, Honour thy father and mother' (v.4). Love never condones an excuse for setting aside our duty to man. So whether we have banjo-playing or drums or an organ or no music at all – if our tradition promotes love, it is not wrong.

Secondly, if it promotes life-giving heart-worship, then it is not wrong. If someone comes into our service filled with fear and in bondage and is set free, then we are not wrong. 'Where the Spirit of the Lord is, there is liberty' (2 Cor. 3:17).

And finally, we know we are not wrong if our tradition promotes conviction of sin. The Pharisees did not have a clue about sin. Everything was external – they thought washing the hands was a mark of good worship. But Jesus said to them, 'Not that which goeth into the mouth defileth a man; but that which cometh out of the mouth, this defileth a man . . . But those things which proceed out of the mouth come forth from the heart; and they defile the man. For out of the heart proceed evil thoughts, murders, adulteries, fornications, thefts, false witness, blasphemies. These are the things which defile a man: but to eat with unwashed hands defileth not a man.' Worship which is by the Spirit leads inevitably to a sense of sin, insight, and a changed life: which results in holiness.

We do not want to be tradition takers, tradition breakers or tradition makers. We only want to be sure that our tradition, whatever it is, is not wrong. Let us therefore allow the Holy Spirit to set the standard because what we want is worship which touches the heart and changes lives. There is no value in anything else.

CHAPTER 22

WORSHIP AND LITURGY

'When ye come together . . . Let all things be done unto edifying.' (1 Corinthians 14:26)

Although it is an over-simplification, one can say that there are two basic styles of worship: liturgical and non-liturgical. In liturgical worship the service is taken from a worship book, such as the Book of Common Prayer. The structure of the service, and the individual responses, prayers and readings suggested in the book are all followed.

I confess that in the past I have been very suspicious of this form of worship. I have always called to mind 2 Corinthians 3:17: 'Where the Spirit of the Lord is, there is liberty,' and have felt that liturgy must mean the opposite of liberty.

But I think I was wrong in my attitude, for I have come to see that there are degrees of structure. Following a planned service can simply mean deciding at which point the collection is to be taken. At the other extreme, it can mean sticking to a rigid order of service, with no possibility of variation. I have also seen that some people need this second type of service. Recently, I was talking to a lady whose husband, a minister, had left her and given up his church. She said to me, 'I made my way one day to an Anglican church. I needed a liturgical worship, where I knew every Sunday would be the same and there would be no surprises.'

The word 'liturgy' comes from a Greek word *leitourgias* or *leitourgos*, which, in the Authorised Version, is almost always translated 'minister', or 'ministry'. This word is used twice in Hebrews 8. In verse 2 it refers to 'a minister of the sanctuary' (*leitourgos*). And in verse 6 the reference is to the 'more excellent ministry' (*leitourgias*) of Jesus. The word means 'serving people', but it can mean 'serving God', and often means ministering to people through the worship of God, for example, in Romans 15:27, where Paul says, 'For if the Gentiles have been made partakers of their spiritual things, their duty is also to minister [*leitourgesai*] unto them in carnal things.'

There is also the reference to Zacharias the priest, father of John the Baptist, of which it is said, 'And it came to pass, that, as soon as the days of his ministration [*leitourgias*] were accomplished, he departed to his own house' (Luke 1:23).

In order to prepare this chapter, I have studied the origin and development of liturgy in New Testament times and through Church history to the present day, and have concluded that there is no such thing as non-liturgical worship. It is a myth to think there is. Every church has its own identifiable liturgy. It takes one form in the Church of England, and another in the Roman Catholic Church. The Pentecostals have their liturgy, and the Charismatics have theirs.

In Chapter 21 I described how I preached one summer for the Coral Ridge Presbyterian Church in Fort Lauderdale, where we wore robes and walked behind the choir down the centre aisle. The opening hymn was chosen to fit the time it would take us to reach our places. At the end of the last verse there I was all ready in the pulpit. I knew also when I must finish preaching.

That evening I preached in Bimini with Bonefish Sam in his freestyle service. Now he would claim that they did not follow a liturgy. But the first thing Sam did that night when he came into the pulpit was say, 'Praise the Lord!' And the people all replied, 'Praise the Lord!' Then he said, 'Say, thank you, Jesus!' And everyone said, 'Thank you, Jesus.' He did it that night, and he'll do it tonight and again next week! That's just as liturgical as the church I was at in the morning.

In my own church we only vaguely follow the church calendar. But nobody would be happy if I were to preach on 'God's judgment and AIDS' on Christmas morning. Or if on Easter Sunday morning I preached on 'The wise men following the star'.

Within our free church services we feel that a more formal liturgy is more appropriate on some occasions than others. The Lord's Supper follows a liturgy which Jesus himself introduced. Many churches follow a written order of service and use set prayers and responses for baptismal services. At a funeral service certain scriptures are normally read, and at the grave side we repeat the words, 'ashes to ashes, dust to dust'. The wedding service is largely liturgical, as are services dedicating babies to God.

Liturgy was God's idea from the beginning. The Law was total liturgy, yet the giving of the Law was from God. The Law is in three parts: moral, civil and ceremonial. The moral law is the Ten Commandments. The civil showed how the people of Israel should govern themselves and get on with each other. And the ceremonial law set out in detail how to worship God. In Exodus, Leviticus, Numbers and Deuteronomy, for example, there are careful descriptions of the Tabernacle, the altar, the shew bread, the candles and the incense; the movements of the priest on the Day of Atonement are carefully prescribed.

Jesus fulfilled the whole law – ceremonial, civil and moral – by his life and by his death. We in turn fulfil it in two ways. One is by substitution. None of us could ever totally keep the Law, but Jesus kept it perfectly. Christ is our righteousness and our sanctification, our wisdom and our redemption. In Christ all of us perfectly fulfil the Law.

We fulfil the Law also by walking in the Spirit, for if we walk in the Spirit we will not obey the lusts of the flesh. This is why worship is to be by the Spirit.

The question for us, therefore, is: does worship in the Spirit negate the need for all structure, and all liturgy, in our personal lives and in our church services?

I would say that the answer is, 'Certainly not!' In the chapter on prayer we have already seen that the presence of the Holy Spirit in the early Church did not prevent Peter and John going to the Temple to pray at a set time of prayer (see Acts 3:1). Even where there is a great measure of the Spirit we need a place and a time to pray. Some people fancy they are so spiritual that they can just read the Bible as they feel led, and pray when they are in the mood. But these people are shallow and know little of the real impulse of the Spirit. We must never think that we can outgrow structure in our own lives. We need a disciplined Bible-reading plan, and not one of us can afford to pray for less than thirty minutes a day.

What are the advantages of liturgy and structure in a church worship service? I would like to name five, although there may well be more. The first is that it enables people to know when to start and where to meet.

Secondly, it sometimes helps people with no Christian background.

Thirdly, it ensures that worship has theological content. Christians who know nothing but a completely unstructured style of worship tend to be theologically and spiritually starved. Some churches would possibly benefit from using set prayers. We have a rich heritage of prayers written by theologically minded, godly people. These prayers would bring far greater blessing than the endless diet of repetitive, superficial chorus singing which in some churches virtually takes up the entire service.

A fourth advantage of liturgy is that it provides a measure of blessing if the minister or preacher is not leading the worship in the Spirit. We may sometimes think, 'I'm not going this morning, the preacher is not a man of God.' But liturgies, prayers and hymns normally have been written by men of God, and God can speak through them, no matter who is leading the service. They also help us to avoid getting into extremes, such as the Quaker idea of just sitting and waiting in the service for the Spirit to move the people.

Another point, is that in these days of waiting for revival, when we often don't feel like praying, it is helpful to be able to fall back on liturgy and structure. Paul said, 'Be instant in season, out of season' (2 Tim. 4:2).

A final advantage of liturgy is that it provides a promise that the service will come to an end. And if the Spirit does not come down in the kind of power one wishes for, it is good to know that the service will stop!

What I have been saying is that God can own a prescribed worship just as much as he can own a prescribed sermon. I myself don't come to the pulpit unprepared. I know most of what I'm going to say before I come — though I may think of some of my stories or illustrations as I go along. I don't read my sermons, but would it matter if I did? In his most powerful sermon *Sinners in the Hands of an Angry God*, preached at Enfield, Connecticut in 1741, Jonathan Edwards took as his text the words from Deuteronomy 32:35: 'Their foot shall slide in due time: for the day of their calamity is at hand.' Before he had finished speaking, five hundred strong men were found outside holding on to tree trunks to keep from falling into hell. Inside they were holding on to the pews, so great was the sense of the Spirit's presence. Yet Edwards had poor eyesight and was forced to hold his manuscript up to his eyes as he read.

We need to be aware of the difference between the

liturgical and the sacramental. When we talk of a service being 'liturgical' we are referring to the outward form only. A liturgical service has no power to transform those who take part. Without the presence of the Holy Spirit, the liturgy is dead. But if a ritual is termed 'sacramental' people are saying that it automatically confers inward grace on the participants. In the Roman Catholic church, when the priest prays over the bread and wine and says, 'Hoc est corpus meum' – 'This is my body' – it is believed that the bread and wine become the body and blood of Jesus. Therefore when you eat them you are eating Jesus and grace is conveyed to you, whether you feel it or not, whether you believe or not.

Though I accept the validity of a liturgical service, I do not accept that a rite or service can be sacramental. When we baptise someone we do not believe that that person is being saved by the simple act of baptism.

There can be disadvantages in slavishly following a liturgy, and I touched on this in the chapter on tradition. It can mean that the service is superficial and mechanical. It can lead people to forget that they must depend on the Holy Spirit, and it can militate against expectancy, and give a self-righteous feeling.

There are, I believe, three principles we should remember when we consider the place of liturgy in our church services. The first is that the aim of liturgy should be the glory of Christ. As Paul puts it in 2 Corinthians 3: 'Nevertheless, when it shall turn to the Lord the veil shall be taken away . . . But we all, with open face beholding as in a glass the glory of the Lord, are changed into the same image from glory to glory, even as by the Spirit of God' (vv.16, 18).

The second principle is that the proof of a valid liturgy (as with a valid tradition, as we have seen) is that it gives freedom. Any liturgy which gives liberty is owned by the Spirit, for 'where the Spirit of the Lord is, there is liberty' (2 Cor. 3:17). And liturgy which is of the Spirit will also produce growth and self-discipline. In 2 Corinthians Paul went on to say, 'Therefore seeing we have received this ministry, as we have received mercy, we faint not' (4:1).

The third principle is that many liturgies are temporary. In God's plan of redemption in the Bible we see a moving away from a set liturgy. In 2 Corinthians 3 Paul says that there are two kinds of worship. Both were given by God, both are called 'glorious', and both had their proper place. One was by the Law, and the other is by the Spirit. Paul describes the former as 'the ministration of condemnation' and the latter as 'the ministration of righteousness' (2 Cor. 3:9). The law may have been glorious, but it had to be 'done away' with (2 Cor. 3:11) and replaced by 'a new and living way, which he hath consecrated for us' (Heb. 10:20). As Hebrews 8:13 puts it: 'In that he saith, a new covenant, he hath made the first old. Now that which decayeth and waxeth old is ready to vanish away.'

There are certain unchanging liturgies, but by and large liturgy is instituted for temporary situations, for the way God wants to be worshipped is by the impulse of the Spirit. We must have discernment to see what is changing and what is unchanging. The Lord's Prayer is an unchanging liturgy, and in the Bible there are timeless blessings which are liturgical in form, for example, Numbers 6:24–26: 'The Lord bless thee, and keep thee: the Lord make his face to shine upon thee, and be gracious unto thee. The Lord lift up his countenance upon thee, and give thee peace.' As we said, the Lord's Supper is an unchanging liturgy.

On the other hand, almost every liturgy which has come down through the history of the Church has been temporary only. The second generation of any church, denomination or movement must beware of keeping up a liturgy which is no longer relevant. Any liturgy which we have inherited should not be accepted uncritically. We must see whether its origin is in something unchanging from the Bible or whether it simply comes from a habit or mannerism or style which was born when the Spirit was present in power and no longer applies. For it is ridiculous to try to keep something up after the Spirit has gone.

We have got to be willing to follow what the Spirit is doing *today*. The impulse of the Spirit is our key, and it must take priority over any changeable liturgy. When Peter and John were on their way to the temple to pray, and met the lame man, Peter stopped and healed him. Imagine John saying, 'Hey, Peter, come on, we've got to be there by three o'clock. They're waiting for us'!

It takes not only spirituality, but courage, to see through an irrelevant liturgy. For we all have our comfortable liturgies. May God help us all to find the liturgy of the Spirit. It won't be written on a little prayer card. There will be no magical formulae to usher it in. It will be dictated by an inward peace which cannot be counterfeited. When the Spirit resides ungrieved in the hearts of a congregation, something will happen which defies a natural explanation, and everyone will know that the new has come. When the Spirit is present, the only thing to do is to step aside and let him have his way. And then there will be liberty and great glory.

CHAPTER 23

THE JOY OF DOING NOTHING

'In returning and rest shall ye be saved; in quietness and in confidence shall be your strength.' (Isaiah 30:15)

So far we have been thinking a great deal about what we can *do* in worship — admittedly in response to the Holy Spirit — but nevertheless our actions of praying, praising, listening, loving and obeying. And of course there is nothing wrong with that. But there is a much deeper level of worship, one in which we are unable to express ourselves verbally or non-verbally — where we are utterly passive. The highest and most intense worship takes place when we can do nothing but be amazed, when we are rendered helpless and speechless with wonder and gratitude, when we just sit back and watch God work. This is what Isaiah is talking about when he says, 'For thus saith the Lord God, the Holy One of Israel; In returning and rest shall ye be saved; in quietness and in confidence shall be your strength' (Is. 30:15).

In worship at this depth we are kept from even saying, 'Thank you.' For, at the risk of being misunderstood, I am prepared to say that our gratitude sometimes gets in the way of praise. Gratitude can be an attempt to get the balance even again. Probably you have experienced on a human level something of what I am getting at. Someone does something for you, and you know very well that he or she wants you to be thankful, and you are, so you express your gratitude. You try to be extremely thankful so that this person will really see how you feel. Or you try to return the favour in some way. This gives you a feeling of satisfaction.

Have you ever been placed in a situation in which there was nothing you could say or do? Someone did something immensely wonderful and you weren't able to do anything but feel grateful? Perhaps the person went away, and you wished you could find him or her to say how much you appreciated what was done. And maybe you felt frustrated, and some of your joy was taken away because it was not possible to express your gratitude. On the natural level, we always feel that we must do something.

But Isaiah says that our salvation lies in the fact that we do nothing: 'In returning and rest shall ye be saved.' I did not say that we feel nothing, but that we do nothing. This, says Isaiah, is the best way to live – the way God wants us to live. It constitutes the greatest joy there is. And even though we are rendered helpless – as though we are just standing there with our mouth wide open – God sees how we feel and knows that we are grateful.

Yet, though this is what God wanted, the people Isaiah was speaking to would not do this. It reads: '. . . in quietness and in confidence shall be your strength: *and ye would not.*' The people wanted to 'do' instead. They said, 'No; for we will flee upon horses . . . We will ride upon the swift.' And that's the way so many of us are. We can't imagine getting satisfaction from anything but 'doing'. We must be always working – always on the go. We feel guilty if we are not on the move.

Isaiah 30:15 is set in the context of a solemn rebuke. The people of Israel thought that they had better ideas than God on how to fight their battles – and they had actually turned to Egypt for help. The chapter begins, 'Woe to the rebellious children, saith the Lord, that take

194

counsel, but not of me . . . That walk to go down into Egypt, and have not asked at my mouth; to strengthen themselves in the strength of Pharaoh, and to trust in the shadow of Egypt!' (vv.1–2). They thought that God would understand if they turned to the resources of Egypt for help to fight his battles. They wouldn't listen when God said, 'This is a rebellious people, lying children, children that will not hear the law of the Lord' (v.9). They only wanted to hear pleasant things. Verse 10 says they were a people 'which say to the seers, See not; and to the prophets, Prophesy not unto us right things, speak unto us smooth things, prophesy deceits'. As a result, although they claimed that they were doing the Lord's work, they were really rejecting the Holy One of Israel.

And the Lord said to them, 'Therefore this iniquity shall be to you as a breach ready to fall, swelling out in a high wall, whose breaking cometh suddenly at an instant' (v.13). They would be destroyed as completely as pottery breaks in pieces: 'And he [God] shall break it as the breaking of the potters' vessel that is broken in pieces; he shall not spare: so that there shall not be found in the bursting of it a sherd to take fire from the hearth' (v.14).

And it is at this point that Isaiah had the boldness to tell the people what God envisaged for them: 'Thus saith the Lord God, the Holy One of Israel; In returning and rest shall ye be saved.' Not in going to Egypt, but in just looking to God and relying on him. 'In quietness and in confidence shall be your strength.' All God asked for was the complete trust of the people. He wanted them to get their joy from seeing him accomplish his word. But they wouldn't have it.

Two Christian doctrines emerge here, the first of which is justification – being made righteous in God's sight – by faith alone. Romans 4:2 says, 'For if Abraham were justified by works, he hath whereof to glory; but not before God.' And verse 5 says, 'But to him that worketh not, but believeth on him that justifieth the ungodly, his faith is counted for righteousness.' So if any of us think we will go to heaven when we die because we've tried to live a good life and haven't done much wrong and haven't hurt anybody, then we must see that we are wrong, and are at this moment on the way to hell. God does not justify us because of our actions or our words. Justification comes simply by trusting in what Jesus did on the cross.

The second doctrine concerns the living of the Christian life. Our Christian life must be lived without confidence in works. I don't mean it's to be lived without works, but it is to be lived without relying on what we do to get God's approval. We must not feel conscious of any good we are doing, but must consider that what we are doing is nothing. Jesus said, 'But when thou doeth alms, let not thy left hand know what thy right hand doeth' (Matt. 6:3). And Paul says in Galatians 2:20: 'I am crucified with Christ: nevertheless I live; yet not I, but Christ liveth in me: and the life I now live in the flesh I live by the faith of the Son of God, who loved me, and gave himself for me.' As long as we are conscious of our works or derive our assurance from them – as long as we are so impertinent as to conclude that we are saved because we do good things – then we grieve the Spirit and cut ourselves off from the joy which can be ours just by trusting in his word alone.

If we are living in frustration and bondage, always checking our spiritual pulse to see whether or not God loves us, and whether we are saved, we show that we are only looking to ourselves. As Calvin said, 'If you contemplate yourself, that is sure damnation.' It is idolatry, for it shows we are not looking to God.

God just wants us to believe his word. And his word says that if we look to him we are saved. 'There is life in a look,' said Spurgeon. 'In quietness and in confidence shall be your strength.'

When we are in heaven singing the praises of God we will know that God did it all from start to finish. But

Isaiah's point is: see this *now*. Live like this *now*. Because that is where our strength in living lies. When some people get to heaven and finally realise that they were saved by grace alone, they will look back and think of all the guilt and frustration they went through here below, all their anxiety and rushing about, all their questioning, 'Am I a Christian?', and will see just how useless it all was.

After years and years of the Christian life many people still worry about whether they are really Christians. But this is of the devil. He tries to paralyse us and keep us looking inward for our confidence. Whereas if we settled it once and for all by trusting God's word, we could get on with our life and with worshipping God.

Isaiah is saying, 'Don't wait until you get to heaven to find out that you were saved all along! See it now and it will change your whole lifestyle. You will see God work in a manner that you never dreamed of!'

I fear also that so much of our worship today is motivated by self-righteousness. We sing our hymns and pray pious prayers and tell God how much we love him. Then we leave the church feeling really good inside – but it makes God sick. We are like the person who talks about himself all the time; he may enjoy it, but everybody else is thoroughly fed up!

Remember that Simon Peter, after he had walked with the Lord for three years, said, 'I will lay down my life for thy sake.' Yet Jesus said to him, 'Wilt thou lay down thy life for my sake? Verily, verily, I say unto thee, The cock shall not crow till thou hast denied me thrice' (John 13:37–38).

We may get a good feeling out of saying, 'Lord, I love you.' But he sees right through us.

Yet the marvel is that Jesus kept right on speaking to Peter. As I have already said, in the Greek there were no commas or full stops, much less chapters and verses. This means that Jesus actually said to Peter, 'The cock shall not crow, till thou hast denied me thrice. Let not your

heart be troubled: ye believe in God, believe also in me'
(John 13:38, 14:1). Here is one who knew what Peter was
going to do, yet he said, 'Let not your heart be troubled:
ye believe in God, believe also in me.'

We are saved through his grace — not by whether we
keep our word of promise to him.

So much of our worship is aimed at getting a good feeling for ourselves. We think we have shown God how
much we love him, or we feel we have paid our dues, as
it were, or have gained some leverage with God by going
to church. But God spoke as he did in Isaiah 30:15
because he wanted the people of Israel to see his total
grace and their total helplessness. He wanted them to see
his power alone.

Do you know the feeling of having fallen and having
been forgiven? If you haven't, then there is a sense in
which you are impoverished. I suppose one of the most
controversial things Martin Luther ever said was his
advice to Melanchthon: 'Sin lustily, that grace may
abound.' Taken out of context, such a statement is
dangerous and can easily be misunderstood. But Melanchthon was a very delicate, self-righteous person who
wouldn't dream of doing anything wrong in a thousand
years. And he wasn't really enjoying the grace of God.
Luther meant that if he were to fall real good, when he
came to God he would feel forgiven and fresh.

But we certainly don't need to fall in an obviously bad
way for that to happen. Sometimes God will just let us see
what is there in our hearts — that inability to forgive, that
need to vindicate ourselves, all that wickedness. And
when we see that God accepts us with all that, it is marvellous. Self-righteous people can never truly worship, for
they have no sense of sin.

Isaiah very much wanted the people to enjoy hearing
the voice of God. The way to do this is through *rest*! 'In
returning and rest shall ye be saved.' Hebrews 4:10 says,
'For he that is entered into his rest, he also hath ceased

from his own works, as God did from his.' And the key phrase here is, 'from his own works'. We need to stop feeling the need to be always on the go. We must stop getting our joy from 'being involved'. If we are frustrated and burnt out, then there is no trust. But when we cease from our work and just do nothing – then we see that God likes us just the way we are – and that is when we worship!

Do we think that we are only important to God when we are doing something? Isaiah says, 'In returning and rest shall ye be saved, in quietness and in confidence shall be your strength.' This is the way God wants us to live. When someone does something wonderful for us, we may not always be able to thank them, and they'll never know how we feel. But with God we can be left in awe, and he does know how we feel. He just wants us to enjoy seeing him do what he by himself alone can do.

This is far more than the first ABC of holy living. Some people are paralysed because they have never got beyond the first steps in sanctification. The first steps are important, but we must move beyond that level. What Isaiah is doing here – and what the Holy Spirit is doing today – is giving each of us an invitation to enter the big league.

'By faith Noah, being warned of God of things not seen as yet, moved with fear, prepared an ark to the saving of his house' (Heb. 11:7a). Noah saw God do marvellous things. Abraham trusted God and got Isaac back. Jacob was a man who had seen sorrow, for he had lost Joseph. He had been a scoundrel from the word go, but he got Joseph back, and at the end of his days he could be found leaning on his staff and saying, 'God is so good.' He knew he didn't deserve anything. He just worshipped. By faith, Joseph saw that his bones would be taken back to Canaan when the nation returned. Moses saw the children of Israel cross the Red Sea on dry land: all he could do was stand in amazement and watch. Joshua in his turn saw the walls of Jericho fall.

And that's how God wants it to be with us. He wants us

to trust and see him work.

But as long as we are always on the go, trying to bring in the kingdom by our activism, God will just fold his hands and say, 'You want to do it? Go on then.' There was a time when Abraham got impatient and ran ahead of God. He had no children, and Sarah was old, yet God had told him that he would have a son. When the child did not come, he lay with Hagar, Sarah's servant girl. And for fourteen years Abraham thought Ishmael was his promised heir.

Then one day God said, 'Sarah will conceive.' And she did, and Isaac was born.

How many of us today have wanted to see God act, and so have fallen into this same mistake of rushing in and making something happen and then calling it the work of God?

Isaiah 30:18 says, 'And therefore will the Lord wait, that he may be gracious unto you, and therefore will he be exalted, that he may have mercy upon you: for the Lord is a God of judgment: blessed are all they that wait for him.'

Have you wondered why God isn't working? It's because you're doing the work. So God says, 'I'll just wait.' And when we run ahead rather than rest, we will always be sorry. When the Israelites said, 'We will flee upon horses . . . We will ride upon the swift,' God said in effect, 'You certainly will run. You'll stay on the run, and your pursuers will be swift. The day will come when you will have to look to me, and I will be gracious then to you.'

Some people are anxious to vindicate themselves – to clear their name from some lie. They meddle here and pull a string there. And God says, 'Oh, you want to do it? Go on, then. I'll just wait.' And they make a bigger and bigger mess of things. Others are trying to fight their own battles or to nudge the arm of God's providence. Well, God said, 'You try that, and you'll be more vulnerable than ever.' Verse 17 says they would be 'left as a beacon upon the top of a mountain, and as an ensign on a hill'. They would be a wide open target for all to see their folly.

Many people can't imagine that doing it God's way – the way of faith alone – could turn things around. Some people are running their business affairs in a way that is dishonouring to God, and they say, 'Well, we live in a wicked world. We just have to do some of these little shady things.' They're frustrated and in trouble because God has folded his arms and said, 'Go on – you try it your way.' But if they would get it right with God, he'd bless them. He may not make them millionaires, but they'll have peace – which is something they don't have now.

Some people, though they are Christians, are looking to the world for happiness. They think that by living with that worldly crowd, or by going to one more cinema or one more pub, they will somehow get satisfaction. And they justify themselves by saying, 'God understands that I have needs.' And God lets them do it – but they don't have peace.

There are two principles here which, if we can grasp them, will result in the kind of worship God seeks of us. The first, as we have seen from Isaiah 30:15 and Hebrews 4:10, is that of operating without any fatigue. This is what happens when we get right with God. We just come to him and do it his way. As the NIV puts it, 'In repentance and rest is your salvation.' Repentance means 'change of mind'. It means saying, 'God got it right. I agree with him.'

How many people are utterly frustrated? They have tried everything and the result has only been fatigue. I was talking recently to a minister who said to me, 'I've had to ask for a sabbatical. I'm burnt out.'

When we don't wait on God, and are always trying to do things ourselves, the result is endless turmoil. But if we really want assurance of salvation, God will knock everything out from under us, until we trust him alone.

To rest in God means that we leave everything to him.

We leave it to him to put us in the right place at the right time, and with the right people at the right time, even in the right financial position at the right time. And why is this the way of no fatigue? Well, it is because we get our approval from the blood of Christ, and not from our works, and because we live by the authority of the Spirit of Christ.

The result is that we live and worship in a state of amazement, awe and admiration: which is the second principle I want us to see from Isaiah 30:15. This is because we believe the promise of 1 John 1:9: 'If we confess our sins, he is faithful and just to forgive us our sins, and to cleanse us from all unrighteousness.' The blood of Jesus washes away our sin as though it had never been committed and a fresh beginning always follows. The result is quietness, peace and ease.

And we have quietness over the most difficult situations. Quietness over our deepest fears. For God says, 'Leave it to me.' We lose the desire to get even with those who have hurt us, and we feel little need to prove ourselves. Brother Lawrence says that he could get his joy from leaning over and picking up a piece of straw from the ground. That is what Isaiah 30:15 is talking about.

Real worship is directed towards one who doesn't want anything from us for what he has done for us. There are no strings attached. God only wants us to trust him. He wants us to experience the joy of doing nothing, nothing but resting on the fact that he loves us. God wants us just to look to him and say, 'Lord, I don't know how much I love you. But I know how much you love me.' Rest on that and let God love you. Then you will stand in awe.

Then to our surprise we begin to hear God's voice giving us clear instructions. As verse 21 of Isaiah 30 puts it: 'Thine ears shall hear a word behind thee, saying: This is the way, walk ye in it.' Note the order: first we rest on the fact that God loves us and then we hear him speak.

It is a way of no fatigue and of continual amazement.

Mr Poole Connor, the man who founded the Fellowship of Independent Evangelical Churches, lived into his nineties and before he died he said, 'The longer I live and the older I get, the more amazed I am that God sent his Son into the world to die on a cross for my sins.'

That's the way we are saved. That's the way we are to live. And that's what will bring true worship by the Holy Spirit.

CHAPTER 24

WORSHIP AND REVIVAL

'And at midnight Paul and Silas prayed, and sang praises unto God: and the prisoners heard them.' (Acts 16:25)

Revival is the sovereign intervention of God – and it is for this that we are all longing and waiting for. When revival comes there will be no more need for books on worship!

But what can we do till then? Do we just wait? Is it pointless to think about worship when we know revival will clarify it and straighten it out? Well, we can do something. As Donald Grey Barnhouse used to say: 'While we wait, we can worship.'

When Paul came to Philippi revival came upon the people there who were seeking God. It started with Lydia, a seller of purple. Luke says that Lydia 'heard us: whose heart the Lord opened, that she attended unto the things which were spoken of Paul'. Three types of worship can be seen here. We could call them traditional worship, transitional worship and transformed worship.

Before Paul arrived, Lydia worshipped God in the traditional way, as she had been taught. She did worship God – but something needed to happen to her. She needed new life. I think this is the way it is with many churches.

When Lydia listened to Paul her worship entered a transitional stage. And I think even more churches are in this stage. Christians in this country are listening, praying and waiting. We are all longing for transformed worship which comes when, as with Lydia, the Lord opens our hearts.

In Lydia we see revival in miniature. But she was part of a wider movement of the Spirit. It is helpful for us to see what happened when Paul came to Philippi, and how he saw revival there.

The worship and revival described in Acts 16 began with an unexpected change of plan. We read in verse 6 that they 'were forbidden of the Holy Ghost to preach the word in Asia'. Whereupon Paul and his companions came to Mysia. They wanted to go to Bithynia, but again the Spirit wouldn't let them. They must have felt very confused, for they had never known anything like this before. There was nothing wrong with what they were wanting to do. No one could argue that their desire to preach the gospel in Asia was wrong. That is true of so much that is traditional: you can't call it wrong, exactly.

All this may have been unsettling and even scary for Paul and Silas. And that is how many of us feel about the whole subject of revival, and why many don't want revival, and hold back on it. People like to have things planned. The unplanned and spontaneous is disturbing and alarming.

It has been said that a great work of the Spirit often begins with confusion, and that to confuse is the first work of the Holy Spirit. Perhaps that is happening to you as you read this book, and you wonder what is going on. Well, it may be that God is up to something great. What should you do? Paul and Silas let God lead them. They obeyed the Spirit. And following upon their obedience there came a vision. We read in verse 9: 'A vision appeared to Paul in the night; There stood a man of Macedonia, and prayed him, saying, Come over into Macedonia, and help us.'

There is no virtue in change for the sake of change. The proof that change is right is that there is fresh vision. I know of churches that have got bored with the way they have been doing things, and introduced changes. But because they lacked a vision from God, they have been worse off as a result of their changes. But how do we know that the vision is of God? Following Paul's obedience to the vision there were conversions, beginning with Lydia. Any vision and change that doesn't lead to conversions has got to be held suspect.

Some years ago a very close friend of mine, Bruce Porter, pastor of a church down in the Florida Keys, asked me for advice about proposed changes in his church. I said, 'The proof that you're led of the Spirit is that there will be conversions like you've never had before. That will be the test. If you don't have them, back off. If you have them, God is with you, because only God can save. A conversion is a seal of God.'

The result for my friend was that they had more conversions than they had ever had, and today I believe church attendance has doubled.

This movement of God which began with unexpected change and led on to conversions, was marked by friendship. The word 'comrade' is used among Marxists and Communists, but they haven't a clue about true comradeship. To find that, we need to look in the New Testament.

Here in verse 15 we read that when Lydia was baptised 'she besought us, saying, If ye have judged me to be faithful to the Lord, come into my house, and abide there'. This was spontaneous friendship and it is one of the characteristics of revival. There is nothing forced or false about the fellowship that comes when the Spirit is present. When the Spirit is moving hearts are knit together and a new fellowship emerges between people who thought they had nothing in common and no natural affinity.

But here in Philippi the worship was paralleled by undesirable competition. In verses 16 and 17 we read, 'It came to pass, as we went to prayer, a certain damsel possessed with a spirit of divination [an ability to forecast the future] met us, which brought her masters much gain by soothsaying: the same followed Paul and us, and cried, saying, These men are the servants of the most high God, which shew unto us the way of salvation.'

What do we do about this sort of undesirable competition? Strange as it may seem, we ought to look at odd people suddenly coming on the scene as a not unhealthy sign, uncomfortable though it makes us feel, because revival has a way of attracting people like this.

Two illustrations will bear out the point I want to make. One you may think is a ridiculous illustration, but it has served as a great lesson for me. I've already written about Bonefish Sam, who is a bonefish guide in Bimini. He is a legend in the Bahamas. All the tourist literature back in the fifties would feature Bonefish Sam who was then only in his thirties. He even made the front page of *Life* magazine. I used to go out with Bonefish Sam, and still do.

He tells this interesting story about how there was one spot where you could always find a lot of bonefish. The trouble was, you couldn't catch them there because little mangrove shoots grew around, and whenever you cast your line, should a fish take the bait, it would catch on the mangrove shoots and break the line. It was so exasperating. One day Bonefish Sam had an idea. He went out and pulled up all those mangrove shoots. There must have been dozens and dozens of them. He cleared the whole area out so that when he went back there again we would be able to catch a lot of fish. But when he went back, there were no fish at all. They didn't return until the mangrove shoots grew back. Trying to weed them out killed the whole thing. That's the first illustration.

The second one is a famous story about Whitefield and Wesley. When Whitefield went to the fields and preached, God came down on him and those around him in power and great things happened. People would shout, they would bark like dogs, they would jerk. Fanaticism, no doubt, was a part of it, and John Wesley, a dignified Anglican, criticised Whitefield for allowing that. He told him to weed it out, and remove what was false. Whitefield wisely replied that if you try to remove what you don't like, you will destroy the real as well. He said that you just have to let it go and leave it to God to deal with.

Here is a verse that I cling to: 'Jesus said, Every plant, which my heavenly Father hath not planted, shall be rooted up' (Matt. 15:13). However, God knows how much we can bear. The girl who was calling out after Paul disturbed him for many days. That shows how patient Paul was. But there came a time when he said, 'Enough is enough,' and he dealt with it. God will show us when we must deal with the sort of thing that militates against his purposes and the working of his Spirit. But we must be careful that when we act it is truly from the Spirit.

The worship was also accompanied by controversy. This happened because Paul cast the devil out of this woman. We read, 'And when her masters saw that the hope of their gains was gone, they caught Paul and Silas, and drew them into the marketplace unto the rulers, and brought them to the magistrates, saying, These men, being Jews, do exceedingly trouble our city, and teach customs, which are not lawful for us to receive, neither to observe, being Romans' (Acts 16:19–21).

Internal difficulties led to external controversy. Paul had dealt with the problem that threatened their worship, and Satan was very angry. As a result, the world outside was now affected. We don't have to worry too much about how to reach the world outside when we are faithful to what is going on internally.

We wish everybody would rejoice when revival comes, but they won't because revival exposes sin. Revival breathes holiness and men don't like holiness. The world doesn't want it. People in the world don't see that sin in the heart must be dealt with before there can be real social changes. One of the curses of the modern Church is that it has become enamoured with the social gospel, and has sometimes become preoccupied with lobbying and trying to get laws passed in Parliament. Social change can take place only when the heart is dealt with.

When Paul healed the demon-possessed girl it hurt the pockets of those who had hired her. I believe that Paul's words, 'The love of money is the root of all evil' (1 Tim. 6:10) are to be taken literally. The devil is stirred up when a person's wallet is touched. It is then you have a fight on your hands. Voltaire, the French atheist who got his greatest pleasure from criticising Christianity, used to say that when it comes to money, every man's religion is the same. We need to think very carefully whether the love of money has a grip on us. You may think, 'That's no problem with me. I don't have any money!' But you may be surprised at how much you cling to the little you don't have!

The over-reaction of these men resulted in false accusations: 'They . . . teach customs, which are not lawful for us to receive, neither to observe, being Romans' (v.21). That was simply not true. Paul's accusers didn't say what the real problem was. When Satan is at work lies spread rapidly and those not on the side of truth believe them. The result was that Paul and Silas were put in gaol.

What then? Do you think Silas looked over to Paul and said, 'What have we done? We can't be in God's will; we're in prison. Maybe we were wrong. We felt that we weren't supposed to go into Bithynia or Asia but maybe we should have gone, Paul.'

Do you think Paul replied, 'I know. We're in prison. We couldn't have been in God's will. When you are in God's will you never have problems. What are we going to do?'

What really happened? In Acts 16:25 we read, 'At midnight Paul and Silas prayed, and sang praises unto God: and the prisoners heard them.' They continued to worship with undaunted courage.

When revival comes you just can't stop people worshipping God. When people are filled with the Holy Spirit the time and the place don't matter. The hallmark of real, fervent worship is spontaneity.

One of the stories that often comes out about true revival is that people don't need as much sleep as they usually need. In the Welsh Revival they would go to church and stay there till the early hours of the morning and get up and go to work and not feel tired.

But more was to come for Paul and Silas. The next thing we see was an unusual coincidence: 'And suddenly there was a great earthquake, so that the foundations of the prison were shaken: and immediately all the doors were opened, and every one's bands were loosed' (v.26). An earthquake just happened to come along at that moment while they were singing praises to God. This coincidence of the earthquake and Paul and Silas worshipping was a seal of the sovereign, glorified God. It is often the case when revival is at its height that extraordinary things happen which defy a natural explanation.

A lot of people say, 'When I see that happen, I'll believe revival is coming.' But when it comes to that stage, those who are still waiting to decide whether it is really a work of God are detached from it to such a degree that they don't get any pleasure from it. There can be a deep weeping and wailing and gnashing of teeth when people see God at work and are left out because at the beginning they held back. 'He that is faithful in that which is least is faithful also in much: and he that is unjust in the least is unjust also in much' (Luke 16:10).

More happened: unexpected conversions. We read that the keeper of the prison woke up and when he saw the prison doors open he drew out his sword to kill himself. He knew he would be held responsible for the prisoners' escape and would be killed in their place. But Paul said, 'Don't be afraid. We're here. Don't hurt yourself.'

Then the gaoler asked an interesting question: 'What must I do to be saved?' This shows that Paul and Silas must have been witnessing to him. How else would a gaoler know about being saved? It's not exactly the sort of language you would expect to hear in gaols. Nor is it language that is much in vogue today. I was talking to a minister recently who said he likes to use the word 'committed'; 'saved' was a bit too holy or too old-fashioned for him – or for many people.

The gaoler and all his family became believers that night. Isn't it wonderful that God should use an earthquake to get to one family? God can do it for he wants to save his own, and he will go to extraordinary means to bring about response.

In this revival in Philippi there was preaching, singing, witnessing, conversions and a touch of the extraordinary. There was competition, controversy, confrontations. Then, finally, there was undoubted clarification. What had begun with change and confusion ended with joy. Looking back, Paul and Silas could see the hand of God in it all.

How is it with us? God puts tests before us. Do we have a clear vision for the lost? Will we panic when we see undesirable competition? Are we afraid of controversy?

I have already mentioned the summer of 1956. It was a very dark time for me. Some months before I had experienced entering into God's rest, and I thought that my family would all be thrilled to bits when they heard of what God was doing in me. I had discovered truths that only God could have shown to me, but my family weren't so happy. A year or so before my grandmother, so proud of her grandson, the first minister in the family, had bought me a brand new 1955 Chevrolet, a beautiful car, but when I began to displease her she took it back. One relative called me a shame and a disgrace to the family. My friends distanced themselves from me.

One Sunday afternoon I remember listening to 'The Old-fashioned Revival Hour', a radio programme with Charles E. Fuller. They were learning a new chorus. The words were: 'Our Lord knows the way through the wilderness, all we have to do is follow.'

If we do this, he will show us what he is up to in our lives, and in our churches.

CHAPTER 25

PREPARATION FOR ULTIMATE WORSHIP

'. . . and after the fire a still small voice. And it was so, when Elijah heard it, that he wrapped his face in his mantle . . .' (1 Kings 19:12–13)

This book has been based on a series of sermons I gave at Westminster Chapel. One evening, as I walked home towards the end of the series, one of the deacons asked me what I thought I had learned from my messages on worship. In reply, I said that not only had I learned that any worthwhile worship is done by the Spirit of God, but that I had come to understand how important worship actually is.

If only every Christian would become more gripped by a sense of the importance of worship, it would make a great difference to our church life and witness. I wonder whether we realise that God not only cares about the kind of worship we give, but really wants our worship? I find it so moving that God should care about my worship of him.

Our natural reaction to this idea is to think, 'Well, worship of God by little old me isn't going to matter to him!' We tend to think that God will take more notice of the worship of more important people, like the Queen, or the Prime Minister or an eminent man of God such as Billy

Graham. When God sees these people at worship, we feel he must say, 'Ah, this is more like it!' Maybe we don't say this in so many words, but isn't it what we so often secretly feel?

Yet running right through the Bible is the theme that God cares about each individual as though there were no one else to care for. Whether you are five years old, or fifty, or ninety years old, God cares about your worship. He is not interested in your status in life, he looks at *you*.

On Palm Sunday when the children were crying, 'Hosanna to the son of David,' the chief priests and scribes didn't like it. But Jesus said to them, 'Have ye never read, Out of the mouth of babes and sucklings thou hast perfected praise?' (Matt. 21:15–16).

There are not many people alive now who were present at the Welsh Revival. But a little while ago I was speaking to a lady who was there when she was a child of six. She lived in London, but when her father heard that revival had broken out in Wales he took her out of school and sent her there. He argued that she could always go to school but she might never see revival again.

She told me that at the peak of the revival, her older brother, who was eight, stood up in the service and began to pray. She said his face shone like an angel, and he prayed on and on until finally their grandfather went up to him and said, 'All right, you can sit down now.' Such was the worship of a child.

You see, not only do so-called unimportant people matter, but God does not care whether or not you are in a strategic position from which to help spread his name. You may sometimes think, 'I'm not going to be able to do anything for God where I am. Why should he show me anything or give me any insights?' But I think I can prove to you that God wants our worship irrespective of our 'usefulness'.

The proof I can offer is the example of Elijah. 'Well, yes,' you may say, 'of course, God would want to show

Elijah something. But I'm not Elijah. Why would God talk to me?'

But what God had to show Elijah came at a time when his work was virtually over and he had nothing more left to do for God. Elderly people, who are now housebound, can recall days when they were of use in the world. Now they feel useless. Other people feel that they have no gift, and are utterly insignificant. Why should God waste his time revealing himself to them when there is no way they can pass the revelation on to help other people? Yet here was Elijah, getting his most profound insight into the nature of God when he had nothing more to do in the world.

1 Kings 19:9 says of him, 'And he came thither unto a cave, and lodged there; and behold, the word of the Lord came to him, and he said unto him, What doest thou here, Elijah?' The text continues:

And he said, I have been very jealous for the Lord God of hosts: for the children of Israel have forsaken thy covenant, thrown down thine altars, and slain thy prophets with the sword; and I, even I only, am left; and they seek my life, to take it away. And God said: Go forth, and stand upon the mount before the Lord. And, behold, the Lord passed by, and a great strong wind rent the mountains, and brake in pieces the rocks before the Lord; but the Lord was not in the wind: and after the wind an earthquake; but the Lord was not in the earthquake: and after the earthquake a fire; but the Lord was not in the fire. (vv.10–12a)

Then come these remarkable words: 'And after the fire a still small voice. And it was so, when Elijah heard it, that he wrapped his face in his mantle' (vv.12b–13).

Elijah worshipped God. What matters to God is not how important we are, or how useful we are. All that matters to him is the quality of our worship. We may ask,

'Why did God not reveal himself in the stillness earlier on?' Could Elijah not have been more useful to God over the years if he had known about true worship when he was young? Why did he only discover what he did about God and himself right at the end of his life?

The answer is that God was preparing Elijah to worship him and to do nothing else. The only thing that was left for Elijah to do was to give his mantle to Elisha, and anoint Jehu as king (1 Kings 19:15–16). This shows us that there is knowledge of God which a man uses for worship and nothing else. In humanistic education it is said that the only knowledge which is worthwhile is utilitarian knowledge. But God showed Elijah something very profound which he never used.

Worship which is pleasing to God has several characteristics, the first of which is insight: the awareness of God which precipitates and inspires the worship. Next there is integrity: the ability of the worshipper to come before God in truth, with his whole self, and no little corners held back. Then there is indebtedness: the sense of our debt to God. As Isaac Watts put it:

> Here, Lord, I give myself away.
> 'Tis all that I can do.

Fourthly, there is a sense of inadequacy: our inability to express the depth of our feelings towards God. Charles Wesley could only say:

> O for a thousand tongues to sing
> My great Redeemer's praise.

And this quality of worship is possible only through the Holy Spirit. You cannot worship beyond the level of your insight. The intensity of your worship reflects the depth of your insight. And you get that insight by the Holy Spirit. A feeling of indebtedness is proof that you realise

215

that your insight is from God. A sense of inadequacy will also determine the quantity, or length of time of your worship. You feel you must keep on trying to express your love and need of God. And this will continue throughout eternity. For we will always be unable to express our debt to God because we are in heaven and not hell.

True worship exposes our imperfection. It matters to God that we should see how imperfect we are. One of the most painful, as well as, usually, one of the last things we discover about ourselves is that we are self-righteous. Elijah was self-righteous. He said to God, 'I have been very jealous for the Lord God of hosts . . . and I, even I only, am left' (1 Kings 19:10). And even after he had heard the 'still small voice', this imperfection was still there. In verse 14 he is saying exactly the same thing: 'I have been very jealous for the Lord God of hosts . . . and I, even I only, am left.'

And God had used this self-righteous man. Elijah was a most extraordinary man. One who could go to a king and say, 'It's not going to rain again for three years – not until I say it will.' It was Elijah who challenged and confronted the prophets of Baal on Mount Carmel in one of the highest moments in the history of world redemption.

It can be a great comfort to us that, as James said, Elijah was 'a man subject to like passions as we are' (James 5:17). God can use us as we are, with all our inadequacies, and lack of understanding. We always think we have to be so well-equipped, so full of knowledge before God can use us in his work here on earth. And that is not true. Heaven will reveal insight after insight about God: knowledge of God for his own sake. And we think, 'If only I had known this before, I could have been more useful to God.'

But God does not necessarily show us things so that we can use them or teach them to others. He does not need men who have great knowledge, or strategic people who have insight. He does not get his pleasure out of great numbers of people knowing this or that. Instead, he loves to reveal the profoundest truth to one person who may be absolutely unknown – or who may never tell it to anyone, much less use it.

It is very important to know this, because it shows us that our greatest joy and pleasure is to be found in God alone. So much of what is pleasurable in this life has to be shared with somebody else in order to be fully enjoyed. Even if we had tea with the Queen, much of the joy would be in sharing what we had experienced. But the joy of being in the presence of God alone is the greatest joy there is, and does not need to be shared.

Suppose you have accomplished every goal you ever wanted to achieve. You have met everyone you wanted to meet, gone everywhere you wanted to go. What's left?

Elijah was like this. He could not have wanted to achieve more. He had been in the presence of the king, he had travelled both inside and outside Israel, and above all, he had lived to see the prophets of Baal destroyed. What was there left for him?

What was left was the inexhaustible God. David put it like this in Psalm 16: 'In thy presence is fulness of joy; at thy right hand there are pleasures for evermore.' The greatest joy there is lies in God. It's not sex. It's not money. It's not drink or travel or a nice car and good home, or the love of our family, or learning, or music. Whatever your age, the greatest joy there is, is to be found in God.

Many young people say, 'Heaven sounds rather boring to me if all we are going to do there is worship God.' But they say this because they have not yet had a taste of his presence. They are living so much at the natural level that they can conceive nothing else. But, as I hope to show in the next chapter, heaven will be an eternal, never-ending, ever-increasing insight into the glory and power, the wisdom and holiness of God. When I was a boy we used to sing a little chorus: 'Every day with Jesus is sweeter than the day before.' That's the way it's going to be throughout eternity.

And so, after he had seen God work in such a powerful manner all his life, Elijah was given a profound insight. He realised that he had a lot more to learn about God. He had discovered that there were still seven thousand true worshippers in Israel. He saw that God had used him even though he hadn't known these things. And he realised that he hadn't needed to know them in order to be of use to God. Finally, he learned that some knowledge of God does not have to be shared with others.

The greatest thing that we can do here below is to worship by God's Spirit. Maybe we will even see that all we do here is but a rehearsal for our worship in heaven. And God may show us something which is just for us, tempted though we may be to tell it to others. Because God cares that we should worship him with a sense of intensity and indebtedness, of inadequacy yet of almost uncontainable joy. That's what God wants. He doesn't need millions. But he wants you and me.

CHAPTER 26

WORSHIP IN HEAVEN

'Behold, I make all things new.' (Revelation 21:5)

I finished the last chapter by saying that what matters to
God is my worship of him. And my worship and knowledge of God is not a means to an end, but an end in itself.
For that is the way I will spend eternity: worshipping God
for God's own sake, and knowing that this brings him
pleasure. That is what will make heaven, heaven.

Isn't this exciting? We are going to heaven. A man said
to me, 'I'm looking forward to worship in heaven.' Sometimes I can hardly wait.

But what about our worship in heaven? Will we still be
worshipping by the Spirit?

The answer is, 'Yes.' This is because in heaven we will
have the Spirit without measure. That is the way it was
with Jesus here on earth (John 3:34). When we get to
heaven we shall see Jesus as he is, and we shall be like
him. So in heaven we will worship perfectly by the Spirit.

And what about preaching – for we have said that worship is the preparation for and response to the preached
word? I don't suppose there will be any preaching in
heaven, but throughout all eternity our worship will be
the response to the preached word, for it is because of
the preached word that we first came to trust Jesus and
to be saved. As Paul says, 'It pleased God by the foolish-

ness of preaching to save them that believe' (1 Cor. 1:21).

If we want to understand something about the nature of worship we must look at John's vision of heaven in Revelation, for there we get a glimpse of true and pure praise and adoration of God. We have already seen something of this: of the singing and joy, the praising and music in heaven. This is not poetic exaggeration. 'Write,' said the angel to John, 'for these words are true and faithful' (Rev. 21:5).

In Revelation 21:5 we read: 'Behold, I make all things new.' That means there will be things that are different about our worship in heaven.

What won't we be doing in heaven? First, there will be no soul-winning in heaven. That is one enterprise that will be finished for ever (though for some Christians it's never started!). I speculate that the angels will remember nostalgically those old concerts and choirs when they sang over sinners that repented. It won't be happening in heaven. All the people that ever lived, however many, billions and billions, will all be for ever in heaven or in hell. There will be no further population growth. There will be no tithing, no intercessory prayer, no warnings.

Secondly, there will be no sin in heaven. John said, 'There shall in no wise enter into it any thing that defileth' (Rev. 21:27). Through the blood of Christ we are saved, first from the penalty of sin, second from the power of sin, but thirdly — and this part is in the future — from the presence of sin. When that day comes we will have perfect bodies. There will be no sin in body, mind, soul, or spirit.

There will be no scoffing in heaven. John tells us that 'the fearful, and unbelieving, and the abominable, and murderers, and whoremongers, and sorcerers, and idolaters, and all liars, shall have their part in the lake which burneth with fire and brimstone: which is the second death' (Rev. 21:8). So in heaven there will be no blasphemy, no rudeness, no shaking of the fist at God, no God-haters. All the former things are passed away.

There will be no teaching on worship. We will fall on

our faces and worship. No one will be self-conscious in heaven. As Robert Murray M'Cheyne put it: we will love 'with unsinning heart'. There will be no competition, no wandering thoughts, no conflicting ideas. We will worship by the Spirit perfectly.

There will be no speculation in heaven. 'For now we see through a glass, darkly,' said Paul. But then there will be no theological speculation, no eschatological speculation, no trying to project how it is going to turn out in the end. You won't worry, 'What is God's will for me? Did I do this right? What is that other person thinking?' We won't want to know, 'Did Paul write Hebrews? Was Matthew's the first Gospel?' Our small and large questions will be answered.

There will be no more sun in heaven. It is interesting that twice in the book of Revelation we are told that there is no need of the sun. All things will be new there. There will be no thorns, no decay, no curse on the land, no earthquakes, nor hurricanes. Heaven and earth will pass away. There will be no moon, no clouds, no worry about weather, no equator, no rotation of the earth around the sun, no change of seasons, no need for central heating, no nuclear energy, no worry about the ozone layer.

There will be no separation in heaven. When Paul addressed the church at Ephesus, he said, 'I know that ye all, among whom I have gone preaching the kingdom of God, shall see my face no more' (Acts 20:25). After he had finished they all knelt down on the shore just before Paul got on the boat and they prayed. They all began to cry. They hugged and kissed him and they grieved because he had said that they wouldn't ever see him again. Most of us remember the grief we felt the last time we saw one of our loved ones or a close friend or a minister who was very special to us. No more sorrow like that. There will not even be tears for lost loved ones. I can't imagine how that will be. I can't understand how heaven can be a place of joy if any of my loved ones were in hell. But it says, 'God will wipe away all tears from their eyes.'

There will be no sickness in heaven. 'And there shall be no more death, neither sorrow, nor crying, neither shall there be any more pain: for the former things are passed away' (Rev. 21:4). No disease. Some people have migraines, others have arthritis and don't know what it is like to tie their shoes without pain; some have cancer or the agony of seeing their loved ones suffer with cancer. It's hard to imagine an existence without pain. There will be no handicapped people, no one with mental illness. 'Behold I make all things new.'

What will there be in heaven? First, restoration. Have you noticed that little phrase in Acts 3:21: 'until the times of restitution of all things'? This means the restoration of what was lost in the Fall. What was lost in Eden will be restored, never to be threatened again. Hebrews 9:23 talks about the heavens being purified. One of the reasons for this is to make sure that there will never again be a revolt.

In heaven we will worship as Adam did before the Fall, with one big difference – we will have something to be thankful for that Adam was not aware of when he was created in the image of God. There was no sin in Adam before the Fall, so he worshipped without sin. But when we get to heaven we will worship with hearts overflowing with gratitude, for we will worship with the knowledge that we are redeemed by the precious blood of Jesus. 'And they sung a new song, saying, Thou art worthy to take the book, and to open the seals thereof: for thou wast slain, and hast redeemed us to God by thy blood out of every kindred, and tongue, and people, and nation' (Rev. 5:9).

John says, 'He showed me a pure river of water of life, clear as crystal' (Rev. 22:1). There will be a flowing river, a tree of life with fruit to be eaten. We will probably be eating and drinking in heaven, because there will be no hunger, no thirst. There will be enough for everybody.

There will be fellowship – 'a multitude, which no man could number' (Rev. 7:9). Even in man's unfallen state

God said, 'It is not good that the man should be alone' (Gen. 2:18). So in heaven there will be restoration of friendships. In our churches there are people who don't speak to each other. But there will be no way you can avoid someone by sitting on the other side of the new Jerusalem – nor will we want to. We will love the people that we feel uneasy with today.

There will be righteousness in heaven. That means transparent holiness, and perfect justice. There will be no miscarriage of justice in heaven, whether by courts, elections, congressional hearings, or bribery. There will be no discrimination, no racial prejudice, no conspiracies, but total fairness. God looks forward to that. Do you think God doesn't care when somebody is kidnapped, or mugged, libelled? But he sees the end from the beginning. He never panics. He can wait for his name to be cleared.

There will be reunion in heaven. I shall see my mother again, my grandparents, my maternal grandfather who taught me to fish. Did you ever hear the song: 'Will the circle be unbroken by and by, Lord, by and by?' Those who were in the circle with us, but are no longer here, will be with us again. We will all be together in heaven. Do you know of some who are not saved now? Do you have a loved one who is not saved? Maybe you are the link in the circle between that person and heaven.

What will heaven be like? It will be revelation. The truth will be equally clear to all then. And best of all, Jesus will be fully revealed. 'Now we see through a glass darkly, but then face to face' (1 Cor. 13:12). We are all going to see him. My Lord and my God. The one who died for me. The one who comes alongside in my darkest hour. The one I love.

There will be rejoicing in heaven. John said that he heard a loud voice saying, 'Worthy is the Lamb that was slain to receive power, and riches, and wisdom, and strength, and honour, and glory, and blessing. And every creature which is in heaven, and on the earth, and under

223

the earth, and such as are in the sea, and all that are in them, heard I saying, Blessing, and honour, and glory, and power, be unto him that sitteth upon the throne, and unto the Lamb for ever and ever' (Rev. 5:12–13). Rejoicing that will never end. Sometimes we experience moments of ecstasy or complete happiness. We say, 'If only this could go on and on and on.' What is so thrilling is that in heaven it will be like that.

> When we've been there ten thousand years,
> Bright shining as the sun,
> We've no less days to sing God's praise
> Than when we first begun.

A million years later will be like the first day. We will discover – I guarantee it – that the joy of God alone is greater than any joy yet known to man. Greater joy than any physical, or sensual or intellectual pleasure. Greater joy than any success or any vindication or any promotion.

And, finally, there will be reverence in heaven: 'They sing the song of Moses the servant of God, and the song of the Lamb, saying, Great and marvellous are thy works, Lord God Almighty; just and true are thy ways, thou King of saints. Who shall not fear thee, O Lord, and glorify thy name? for thou only art holy' (Rev. 15:3–4). No intimacy with God, no knowledge of him, will diminish the fear, the awesomeness and reverence we will feel.

I don't know all we will be doing in heaven. But I do know we will worship God and the Lord Jesus Christ without any sin and without any self-consciousness. We will worship spontaneously, by the Holy Spirit, without any limitation or hindrance whatever.

May God give us a taste of worship like this while we still have the opportunity to respond to the preached word. We only have one life and it will soon be past. And only what is done for Jesus – in love and worship and gratitude – will last.